GAME WORKING TERRIERS & TERR

SEAN FRAIN

BULL GHYLL PUBLICATIONS

1: WORKING TERRIER ESSENTIALS:

As I am sure we all know by now, the working of terriers today is restricted by the Hunting Act in England and Wales, but still, when any working terrier is loose in the countryside the very first and most obvious essential is a fitted locator collar and locator box. Our working breeds of earth dog do not know of man's ridiculous, unworkable laws and will follow their natural instinct to hunt wild animals such as foxes and mink. It is quite simply impossible to stop them from doing so, thus terriers will get to ground on fox if they are inclined to go to ground and in the interests of animal welfare it is vital to own and use a locator. True, terriers will often get to ground and simply bolt a fox and follow it out, but there will be times when the fox won't bolt, or it cannot bolt because of being held at a tight stop-end, so one will have no choice but to dig your terrier out.

Gone are the days when terriermen located their workers by ear, usually ear to the ground while everyone remained silent, which reminds me of a tale told to me by the late John Cowen, who bred a very game strain of

Lakeland terrier originally based mostly on Willie Irving's bloodlines. Irving had retired as huntsman of the Melbreak Foxhounds but was out hunting with them shortly after his retirement and a fox had been run to ground. Charlie wasn't for bolting, so John Cowen began trying to locate the terrier, while a big chap who was stood watching was making a "ell of a din." Willie Irving turned up and, being very experienced at locating terriers to ground on fox, began helping Cowen, who admitted he learnt much from Willie Irving.

The big chap carried on making a lot of noise and in the end Irving's patience reached its limit. He suddenly rounded on the big chap and told him to "shut it" in no uncertain terms. The fella did exactly as he was told and Irving was soon able to locate the terrier.

When having a locator collar on a terrier, the worry is that in such a situation the terrier owner may be accused of intentionally going out to put their terriers to ground with a view to digging foxes, but intent would have to be proved and the truth is that even when rabbiting it is wise to have a locator fitted, as foxes will sometimes dig into rabbit warrens, or some warrens are big enough to allow smaller terriers access and in tight rabbit holes the risk of them getting stuck is very real.

Johnny Richardson and Willie Irving are just two famous huntsmen and terriermen that had terriers trapped to ground after they got into tight warrens after rabbits, their terriers being got out after several days. I myself have had to dig terriers out of tight rabbit holes after they have tried to get up to a small fox in such places, becoming tightly wedged and unable to move, so fitting a locator collar even when rabbiting is the best thing for the terrier. If a fox is found by the terrier and the terrier is trapped in the process, then having a collar fitted will almost guarantee a successful rescue. Also, a locator collar will greatly speed up the rescue of a trapped terrier, which is only good for their welfare.

The late Tim Poxton, as good a terrierman as one could wish to meet and who had much success in the field and in the show ring with Sam and Bella, two Arthur Nixon bred Jack Russell terriers, was called out to rescue terriers on a number of occasions, but usually no locator collar was fitted and so some of the trapped terriers were never recovered, in spite of Tim's best efforts. It is in the interests of animal welfare that locators are still considered as essential equipment for the working terrier where there is a risk of it getting to ground, or when and where terrier work is legal.

Roy Pilling and I learned how to work terriers together and we both located using the ear to the ground method, a method I have to admit that I used for years simply because I could not afford to purchase a locator set, but, once I had the money, I began using them and was impressed with how much this superb piece of technology speeded up digs and rescues.

Another working terrier essential, in my view anyway, are couplings, which help the terrierman to better control his earth dogs, though when coupled together and loose, be careful that your terriers do not get into dense undergrowth and especially to ground, as one of them could easily choke to death if snagged on something.

Willie Irving hunted the Melbreak Foxhounds from 1926 to 1951 and he always used couplings in order to keep his terriers under better control. This prevented them from being tempted to chase and worry sheep, but it also stopped them from sneaking away and going to ground unseen. During a hunt two of his coupled terriers got over-excited and went off after a fox, falling over the edge of a crag and landing in a nearby tree, the couples snagging with a terrier hanging from each side of a branch. They would have choked to death for certain, had not the branch snapped and the terriers fallen onto a soft couch of heather below the crag. They were unharmed, though a little shaken, so the use of couples can be hazardous on rare occasions, thus the terrierman needs to be careful and attaching a lead to couplings will no doubt be necessary in places, such as in the vicinity of a badger sett. Badger setts are usually quite large and a brace of coupled terriers could get to ground together if they are not put on a lead.

Two of my coupled terriers, actually it was Ghyll and Bella, once got into a rockpile used regularly by foxes, but fortunately the sloping entrance narrowed to a very tight bend and so they could not get fully in while coupled together, so I was able to retrieve them safely, much to my relief. This taught me to always attach a lead to couplings when near any earths likely to be in use.

Suitable digging equipment is obviously an essential when carrying out legal terrier work, or terrier rescues, but other equipment is also essential, such as a good eye wash that will provide much relief to a terrier that has been to ground and has got soil or sand in its eyes, or one that has picked up small bits of debris whilst working dense undergrowth, as well as some salt water for treating cuts or bites, or better still Hibbiscrub, which is superb for cleaning injuries. Such things can be carried in a small bag, or kept in the car. And for the terrierman who works high country such as fell and moorland, I would also strongly recommend that they carry a compass in the event of dense mist descending. I was once lost in a snow blizzard and, on another occasion, I was lost after dense mist dropped, so I invested in a compass so that I could get to lower ground on such occasions. I have never been lost since.

A good towel is also another essential. Some may scoff at this, but if you do not dry your working terriers after a long day at work, you risk joint and muscle problems in later life. I can assure you that such diligence extends the working life of your earth dogs. I always give my working dogs a good rub down at the end of the day, keeping a towel in the car for the purpose, and my terriers and small hounds have often worked for more than ten seasons, with some working for as many as thirteen seasons, with a lighter load of course. Bracken, my small, crossbred hound, has just finished his twelfth season and remains in great shape. I am hoping he will carry on for at least one more season. Our workers deserve the very best treatment and the above are just a few essentials that will help the terrierman to get the most out of his working terriers.

2: WORKING TERRIER RESCUES:

During and immediately after the Second World War the fox population increased dramatically and as a result farmers suffered often large losses of their livelihoods to fox predation, lamb and poultry losses causing much worry among the farming communities of Britain. The Yorkshire Dales suffered some of the highest losses of livestock to foxes and hounds were used as gun packs to try to provide some protection for farmers.

Arthur Iveson, mentioned in Plummer's *The Fell Terrier* and known locally as 'Molly-Art' Iveson in order to differentiate him from his father, and possibly others in the area of the same name, joined the armed forces, but was sent home to the Dales in order to carry out fox control because the numbers of livestock losses had rocketed due to a lack of gamekeepers on the land. Wildlife had suffered, particularly ground-nesting birds, and the chicken population, which the nation was depending on for its eggs, suffered terribly after the fox population exploded because few carried out any measures of control at that time.

The government recognised that fox numbers had to be drastically reduced if the nation was to avoid being starved into surrender and so several expert fox controllers were sent home in order to deal with this problem. Arthur Iveson was among the foremost of these as, before the war broke out, he had earned an incredible reputation as a foxhunter of the highest calibre.

On returning home to Aysgarth in 1942 Arthur Iveson, together with such legendary foxhunters as Cyril Breay and Frank Buck, as well as local farmers, set up the Dales Fox Extermination Club. This club set about reducing fox numbers and they were incredibly successful, having accounted for 1'363 foxes using terrier and gun, with John Outhwaite of Bainbridge and Fawcett of Bishopdale being just two of the many farmers they provided an essential service for. In fact, Fawcett lost 40 lambs during the spring of 1947 and a total of 150 were killed by foxes in Bishopdale alone, that year.

This kept Iveson and the others very busy in the spring of 1947 and Iveson alone had killed 72 foxes with terrier and gun by June of that year, with several killed at Bishopdale, the brushes of which hung in the outhouse of Rosemary Cottage, Kettlewell, no doubt in readiness of claiming bounty money on them.

The Lunesdale Foxhounds also continued to hunt and usually visited the Dales for a fortnight of hunting every season. They often met at the Board Hotel, Hawes, before making for the fells. In November 1956 Walter Parkin was asked to bring his Lunesdale Foxhounds to the Dales in order to hunt a fox that had been killing large numbers of poultry. Hounds ran a fox into a Shake Hole on Wether Fell in Wensleydale and Walter entered one of his best terriers to deal with it. This was Jock and he was three years of age at this time and was already an outstanding worker.

The report I found does not provide details of what happened to the fox, but when to ground Jock got into trouble and became trapped. Walter Parkin led what proved to be a five-day rescue and Frank Buck, together with many others, provided expert assistance. Twenty-tons of rock was removed during the dig and Jock was located at a depth of sixteen feet and a further six feet into the fellside. He was finally reached on the fifth day of incredibly arduous digging and was well enough, in spite of his lengthy ordeal. Celebrations were held at the local inn.

Just three months later Jock was at the centre of yet another terrier rescue, this time in Barbondale, 2'000ft up Barbon High Fell where hounds had run a fox to ground. Barbondale is a narrow valley which lies between the Lune Valley and Dentdale; a place where Cyril Breay worked his terriers often. Jock was put in and in typical fashion he quickly killed his fox and became trapped once again, the carcass of the fox preventing Jock from exiting the earth. Walter Parkin, Jock's owner, led yet another difficult rescue through earth and rock and it took hard toil lasting a total of 73 hours before Jock and the dead fox were finally reached. Jock was a black and tan terrier bred from Albert Benson's Red Ike line, old Ullswater lines and Cyril Breay's strain. He was incredibly game, a great finder and fox killer and was trapped to ground on several occasions.

At the end of October 1928, hounds ran a fox to ground at a colliery in the Rhondda Valley and terrier Gyp, a fox terrier, was entered. Gyp bolted the fox from this difficult spot, but failed to emerge afterwards. Digging commenced and after a lot of effort Gyp was found trapped behind a rock fall which must have occurred during the tussle with Charlie. Collier manager Eyra Morgan was called in to assist and on the fifth day he led blasting operations which at last freed the trapped terrier. Gyp was very weak and was rushed down to the colliery office, where warm milk and a thick banket soon revived her.

The following must be one of the longest stints to ground ever recorded. In 1953 two Border terriers were lost near Skipton in North Yorkshire and it wasn't until sixteen days later that they were finally located and rescued. The report doesn't provide much in the way of details, but I cannot help wondering if Frank Buck played a part in searching for and rescuing this pair of terriers?

During the month of April 1935, the Ullswater Foxhounds ran a fox into a crag earth and Judy, a fell terrier bitch belonging to one of the joint masters, followed, to bolt the fox. However, Judy became trapped in the earth and so miners helped with attempting to dig her out. Many of these miners were experts with dynamite, but even after seven days of blasting Judy was still stuck to ground and the morale of the rescuers was at a very low ebb by this time, as one can imagine. In fact, it seems most had given up hope of ever reaching Judy, but Patterdale farmer John Teasdale, brother of Tom Teasdale who had been awarded several medals for rescuing terriers and sheep from the surrounding mountains, went alone on the eighth day and managed to free her.

Tina was a working terrier that ran with the Probus Beagles in Cornwall, which were owned by Frank Coombe of Foxleigh, Probus, his kennel maid being Blanche Brown at the time; March 1962. During hunting Tina wandered off, undoubtedly having picked up the scent of a fox and then having followed it into an old mine working. It was soon discovered that Tina was at the bottom of a shaft, 70ft down, but thankfully the mine was dry. An officer from Cornwall Fire Service attended the scene and he was lowered to the bottom of the shaft with ropes. Tina was then brought out to safety and went on to run with beagles many more times.

In May 1930 Hector McDougall, John McLeish, Andrew Falian and James Smith were out hunting for a livestock killing fox and they entered their terrier at a cairn (rockpile) in the Scottish mountains. It was soon obvious that the terrier had got into difficulties and so digging was started, but this was no easy earth to work and they were forced to dig a tunnel through the rocks, by loosening and removing any rocks they could. In fact, the cairn was such a bad place to work that it took them twelve days to reach the place where their fox terrier was stuck, on a ledge by a deep hole in the rocks. McDougall was lowered in and he fetched the terrier out, weak and thin after such a long ordeal, but generally in good shape.

Many miners kept terriers and collieries themselves were often good places for a spot of ratting. 'Bob Jones' was a well known Coleford terrier, famous for his antics after rats, but one day, in March 1926, while chasing a rat, he fell down Margaret Shaft at the pit, falling 24ft where he landed on a ledge. The miners rallied and two shaftsmen were eventually lowered down, effecting a rescue after the terrier had been stuck there for twenty hours.

In October 1928 the famous Blencathra Foxhounds with Jim Dalton late in his hunting career, hunted a fox and ran it into a rock hole at Buckcastle, St John's-in-the-vale. Ernie Parker was whipping-in at the time and he put in his renowned worker, Turk, which made his way deep into the earth, finally working his way up behind the fox. Reynard quickly slipped through a very narrow passage in the rocks and bolted, but the larger Turk was unable to follow, neither could he return the way he had come, probably because he had squeezed into a very narrow part of the earth in his eagerness to reach his fox, but lacked the room to get back out. For two days the hunt followers tried their utmost to dig to Turk, but huge rocks hampered progress, so on the third day local miners began blasting operations. The mining family Stuart, led operations and for three days blasting continued, in order to make a way into this rocky fortress of an earth, till at last Turk could be seen at the bottom of a hole they had made into the rocks. One of the Stuart Miners was lowered by his legs and he managed to grab Turk and both were pulled to safety, Turk having been trapped for five days in all. The number of rescues that have occurred in the Lake District alone would fill a huge volume if they were all recounted and published. This incredibly beautiful part of the British Isles is truly a hard land, a place that has produced hard hunting hounds, game working terriers and tough hunting folk.

April 1950 saw the Head Gamekeeper of the Walshaw Estate, Fred Sayer, a moorland estate near Hebden Bridge, out after a troublesome fox and Rascal was put into a rock hole that the terrier had marked. What followed was a long, hard dig lasting eight days in all, with two miners, the estate keepers and friends helping from dawn till dusk each day, with some days seeing ten diggers on site. An incredible eighty tons of rock was dug out and removed during the rescue, all of the team being determined to succeed, though some days progress was very slow and the outcome far from certain. But finally, on that eighth day, Rascal was pulled from that death-trap earth and survived his ordeal.

February 1938 witnessed the Haydon hunt running a fox to ground at Crag Lough, near Bardon Mill in Northumberland. Tarzan was a smooth fox terrier that ran loose with hounds and he entered what proved to be a natural rock shaft. This was yet another nightmare earth and the work was slow, with blasting operations succeeding in shifting thirty tons of rock before Tarzan was finally reached on the fifth day. He was bitten, but generally in good condition. The report didn't mention anything concerning the hunted fox, but it is my guess that it was successfully bolted.

In 1950 Sam Bancroft of Haworth in West Yorkshire, one-time home of the famous Bronte' family, was carrying out fox control for local gamekeepers when his two terriers, Dandy and Mick, chased a fox into a big rockpile on Cullingworth Moor and it wasn't long before it became obvious that both terriers were trapped. After quite a time of being stuck below ground, a Mister Cockbain, the gamekeeper at Oakworth, turned up and entered his terrier, Brindle. After about an hour of working through the narrow passages among the rocks, Brindle finally emerged and Dandy came out behind him, much to Sam Bancroft's relief, though Mick could still be heard deep down in the rockpile. Dandy was bitten, which told the tale of his game work at this fox, and by now heavy rain had set in, which made the digging rather difficult. Dandy had been to ground for two days, but it was to be after about 72 hours below ground when the other terrier, Mick, was finally got out, after a mammoth effort to dig this bad place.

It is good to know that in 1952 there were still some excellent working Cairn terriers around, one such being named Mack, which belonged to a gamekeeper on the Abbeystead Estate in North Lancashire named Simon Hunter. This same Simon Hunter was good friends with Cyril Breay and the pair hunted regularly together, living only a few miles apart. Hunter lived at Tarnbrook and Cyril Breay at High Casterton on the edge of Kirkby Lonsdale. In fact, Breay hunted on the Abbeystead Estate with Simon Hunter and during the 1960s Breay was accidentally shot while bolting foxes to guns with his terriers, his injuries resulting in a short stay in hospital, but thankfully Breay recovered.

Mack followed a fox into a crevice on Hell Crag situated on the wild moors of North Lancashire and later he became trapped deep inside this rocky lair. Digging commenced, but this was a bad place to work and blasting operations were resorted to, as pick and shovel can do very little when attempting to dig terriers out of some of the more formidable rock dens of the north.

After four days of digging, blasting and clearing tons of rock and clay, the workings became rather unstable and so the blasting was stopped and the rescue attempt abandoned, but Simon Hunter was made of stern stuff and on the fifth morning he returned to Hell Crag with one of the other gamekeepers. They continued to dig by hand and eventually cleared enough rock to make an opening into the rocks. Simon Hunter crawled inside and after quite a struggle the passage widened into a cavern and Mack crawled into the cavern and greeted his master. Mack was weak, but was back at work with his master only two days later. Cairn terriers could obviously still work well and were hardy enough to quickly recover after five days to ground at fox in a very bad place.

 I am sure it is by now well known that working Scottish terrier blood entered the Breay/Buck strain of terrier at some point, but might it also be the case that either Breay or Buck, or perhaps both, also used working Cairn terriers on their strains of terrier? Prick ears are certainly common in modern Patterdale terriers, as they were in both Breay and Buck bred stock, so it is entirely possible that Cairn terrier was used as an outcross at some point. It may even have been Mack that Breay used to bring into his strain of earth dog, as Mister Breay certainly appreciated any terrier of good quality. Certainly, a number of both Breay and Buck bred working terriers looked as though a touch of Cairn blood was present and I believe that Kitty (an incredibly useful worker in deep and dangerous rock holes), Cyril Breay's best worker according to himself, had prick ears.

3: WORKING TERRIERS & OLD DRIFT MINES:
Britain is literally honeycombed with old mine workings, many of them drift mines (usually dug into the ground in such a way so as to avoid the need for expensive pumping equipment) dug by farmers and the owners of country inns who wished to save money on coal supplies, while some even sold coal to local villagers, which means that such places, several of them used by foxes for shelter and breeding purposes, can be a threat to the welfare of our working terriers.

 A large number of these drift mines were dug out on the moors and fells and some of these places are keepered, so putting a terrier to ground for the purpose of protecting wild and reared game birds is legal, but the terrierman would have to think long and hard before working such places. True, if, like myself, one had spoken to a lot of the older generation of terriermen such as the late Brian Nuttall, you would undoubtedly have heard of some great and successful experiences working drift mines with terriers, and

Brian Nuttall certainly enjoyed massive success when putting his Patterdale terriers into drift mines during the 1950s and 1960s in particular, when a lot of old drift mines, though unused, were still open and in generally good repair. Brian took large numbers of foxes from drift mines and lost very few terriers, as he was always careful about where he entered his charges.

Clifford Yates, Nuttall's cousin and another very good, experienced terrierman, has also enjoyed great success at working old drift mines. Scotty was one of Clifford's best terriers and I can remember on several occasions seeing Clifford out hunting with this black and tan terrier many years ago. Scotty could work foxes out of the deepest of old mines, but again, in those days mines were relatively safe to work with terriers.

I myself have worked several old mines around East Lancashire and my bitch Rock became a first-rate finder after working old drift mines and bolting several foxes from such places, but that was during the mid to late 1980s and into the 1990s (I also worked Pep, Bella and Ghyll in old mines, with much success. During the 2000s Mist and Turk got into an old drift mine by accident and bolted two foxes, getting out safely soon after doing so). Nowadays I would be very wary of working old drift mines with terriers, simply because they have been abandoned for decades now (some were still worked as late as the 1960s, even the 1970s in a few cases, though the majority probably haven't been worked since the 1920s or earlier) and so they have deteriorated to a large degree, compared with what they were like during the 1980s.

The old miners used timber as props for the tunnel roofs, or they left pillars of the rock they dug through at regular intervals. Such props and rock supports kept these tunnels relatively safe for many decades, but nowadays those timber props are severely rotted and the rock pillars worn and weakened by every fall of heavy rain, so it is very risky indeed to enter terriers into such places. Brian often went into old mines and sometimes succeeded in finding and fetching out his terrier, which was rather a risky and dangerous business even in the 1950s and 1960s, but these days it would be lethal to enter these old drift mines. Not only are there dangers from what has already been discussed, but poisonous gases trapped in pockets in these mines also pose a threat to terrier or human alike. Also, if a terrier did become trapped, then it would be in danger of drowning if heavy rain set in, as some of these old mines do flood, the drainage channels having long ago become blocked with debris. Brian Nuttall lost Turk, one of his best workers, in a flooded drift mine on the Holcombe moors in the West Pennines.

Brian Nuttall and I discussed this subject on a few occasions and it was fascinating listening to Brian's accounts of his days on the East Lancashire moors with his working terriers (Brian and I had worked many of the same earths, just several years apart). Often Brian would put a terrier in and several hours later there was no sign of it, though two or three foxes may have been bolted. He has then entered the old mines with a torch and has sometimes seen a fox in the passages and his terrier in hot pursuit. In fact, Brian used the old mines for the entering of many of his novice terriers as it taught them to use their noses, cultivating and perfecting that essential finding quality. Also, they chased foxes around these old tunnels before bolting them and this, he believed, really helped bring them on as workers, as it fired-up their enthusiasm for working foxes.

While I would not personally recommend working drift mines with terriers these days, after decades of decay and neglect, I think it fitting to discuss a few of Brian Nuttall's experiences when working such places with his famous strain of Patterdale terrier. Cyril Breay and Frank Buck worked old drift mines, some of them once being coal mines or even slate mines, with considerable success and Nuttall's strain is very much based on old Breay and Buck bloodlines through mostly Kipper, Black Davy and Rusty, so his stock has great breeding for the working of such vast earths.

I have already mentioned Nuttall's Turk, a Patterdale/Jack Russell cross, which was put into an old drift mine in the Holcombe area of East Lancashire. Turk killed his fox, but became trapped. Brian could hear him for three or four days, but heavy rain set in and poor Turk drowned when the mine flooded. His famous Penny, a bitch which bred many great workers, was lost to ground in this same mine for an incredible three week stretch, living on the carcass of the fox she had killed and drinking from water dripping down through the rocks, before Brian finally rescued her.

If any reader does decide to work old drift mines with their terriers, legally of course, and that is surely a personal decision each terrierman must make, then Brian gave me some useful tips, one of the best being not to work them too regularly. He generally found that working a mine just once a month during the hunting season meant that foxes would continue to use such places. If he worked them more regularly, then foxes stopped using these dens, simply because the scent of terriers can linger for some time. It is the same principle with any earth. They all need resting, so that foxes will use them again and again.

Old drift mines certainly hold foxes on a regular basis and if foxes cause problems, as they often do, especially on hill farms, then one may have no choice but to work such places. If so, always use a locator collar and do your best to keep within the law, shooting bolting foxes when possible and safe to do so. I used to wait outside drift mines with lurchers, or a gun when one was available, but the use of lurchers is now outlawed in some countries, so bolting to guns may be your only option. Lurchers, of course, make great fox catchers where legal to use.

4: BAD WEATHER & THE WORKING TERRIER:

Global warming has been having a definite effect on our weather patterns during more recent years, perhaps for the past couple of decades or more, and this unsurprisingly presents certain dangers to working terriers, which are naturally inquisitive and inclined to creep inside any lair into which they can squeeze. Of course, while terriermen try to keep within the law, it is impossible to stop terriers getting to ground altogether, so it is good to be well informed as to the dangers our little tykes face.

Heavy rain is far more frequent these days and this, particularly if coupled with thawing snow, is one of the greatest threats to our working terriers when to ground. Brian Nuttall once told me about a terrier he dug to many years ago, which was in a drain working a fox. Upon breaking through, Brian and his digging companion discovered that the poor terrier had drowned, due to the rain and thawing snow that had built up inside. Snow itself can also present problems, and not just in recent times.

During the late 19th century Joe Bowman, legendary huntsman of the famous and renowned Ullswater Foxhounds, had just finished a week of hunting at Mardale, during the famous Mardale Shepherds Meet held in November of each year in those days, and snow began falling quite heavily. Joe wished to get his hounds back to kennels at Patterdale and so, knowing he would be snowed-in if he delayed any longer, set off on foot with his pack and little shaggy terriers following, but the snow soon began getting deeper and deeper, the air colder and colder until, as he crossed the High Street Range 'twixt Ullswater and Haweswater, he was really struggling and actually started to fear for his own safety.

Two terriers accompanied him on this arduous journey home and the snow was eventually too deep for them to continue on. Joe had become exhausted by this time and so, reluctantly, he was forced to choose which of the two terriers he would be forced to put on the ground and leave behind. Having no other options, as he was too exhausted to continue carrying both terriers, he dropped one of them and, broken-hearted, resumed his travels home, eventually reaching kennels safely. The poor terrier was trapped in the deep snow and sadly died, its corpse being recovered once the snow had melted to some degree. It is thus wise not to venture out in heavy snow and certainly avoid putting terriers to ground in certain earths at such times, such as drains, which will carry off the water after a thaw, which can set in very quickly indeed. Of course, heavy snow can set in during the course of a hunting day and I myself was once caught in a snow blizzard when I was right out on the middle of a wide, sweeping moor and I was soon hopelessly lost (I have been caught out a few times in heavy snow, but have usually been lower in, such as on a country lane, or among woodland, where it is easier to find your way back).

There had been some light snow around on high ground and the weather was very cold generally, but still the lowering cloud and relentlessly heavy snow driven by a strong wind that blew up seemingly without warning, was rather unexpected. I was headed for a good fox holding rockpile on the edge of an old quarry, with two terriers and two running dogs following, but I became disorientated very quickly, as the white-out obliterated everything from view. I marked the general direction of the old quarry as the blizzard was setting in, but still, I hadn't a clue as to where it was within just a few seconds. It just so happened that I landed right by the rockpile after battling my way through the snow, resembling a snowman accompanied by his snow-dogs. I landed too near the rockpile as it turned out, because a fox had indeed taken sanctuary among the rocks and Pep and Rock were loose, so they shot in among the stone piles and very quickly bolted their fox out the other side, before I could get the running dogs organized. The snowfall was abating somewhat, but still, the fox had a good head start and the snow hampered the view of the two running dogs, Bess and Merle. Reynard slunk away and disappeared amongst the white billowing hills long before he was in any real danger of being caught. Had I not chanced upon that rockpile, I would not have put the terriers in until the snow had stopped, but Sod's Law dictated the situation and thus our fox ran on for another day.

Rockpiles generally are safe to work in most conditions, though hard frosty nights and arctic days do present some risk to a terrier working among the cold stones, particularly if it gets into trouble and cannot get out. Many years ago, when working with the Pennine Foxhounds, Paul Stead's excellent working bitch, Tigger, died during a very cold night when she was trapped in a rockpile high in the hills of the South Pennines. A rockpile made up of loose boulders will always be a cold place to work, so terriers with good dense jackets are better equipped to cope in such circumstances.

Getting back to heavy rain, there are numerous experiences of digs taking place against the clock, so to speak, particularly in drains, after rain had set in and the water level in the drains began to rise. A terrier unable to get out during spells of heavy rain is in great danger, so it is always a good idea to check the weather forecast for at least the next two or three days before going hunting. If heavy spells of rain are forecast, then be choosy and very careful about where you put a terrier. Particularly be careful about working drains in low-lying land and avoid coastal or river flood plains during wet weather, for obvious reasons. In fact, I would not work earths in coastal flood plains at all due to rising tides presenting a serious threat to a trapped terrier.

Drains have made up a huge part of my terrier work and I have dug or bolted countless foxes from such places, as the areas I have hunted around Lancashire are littered with them and they hold foxes well, particularly stone drains that are dry in all but the worst of conditions, so it is annoying not to be able to work them where and when it is legal to do so, but when it is unwise to do so because of bad weather.

5: TOUGH WORKING TERRIERS:

To say that the life of a working terrier is hectic is, I feel, rather an understatement, as terriers have had to work foxes out of some very deep and dangerous earths, drift mines being just one type of what is often referred to as an "impossible" place. While it is true to say that we in the north have some very bad places that have to be worked by terriers if effective pest control has to be carried out (some of the rockpiles and borrans in many northern regions have to be seen to be believed and I have frequently been extremely worried about my terriers when they have gone to ground in such places), it is also a fact that countrywide there are difficult and dangerous earths foxes frequent.

While terrier work is restricted by laws made and enforced in ignorance in some countries, terriers can still be used to ground in certain situations in England and Wales, such as on shoots where game birds are reared, for the preservation of such stock. In such circumstances terriers can legally be used to flush or bolt foxes to guns, or, indeed, birds of prey which are capable of taking foxes (two terriers can be used to flush foxes to guns, while, for some inexplicable reason, a pack can be used to flush foxes to birds of prey – a great example of the ignorance of such a law). And so it seems fitting to discuss what can still often be a hectic life for our game little terriers.

One of the best examples of this concerned a terrier belonging to Tom Robinson, the one-time whipper-in at the Ullswater and Melbreak

Foxhounds, Tom's claim to fame being that he it was who first entered Joe Wear's famous Tear 'Em to fox, digging to this dog several times after this. Tom owned a terrier called Rags which was a superb worker. One day in 1943 hounds ran a fox in at Helm Crag above Grasmere and Tom put in Rags. He quickly killed his fox, but got into difficulties and a hard four day dig followed, but then the roof of the dig fell in and a forty foot hole suddenly appeared – what is known as a sink hole – and it was thought Rags was lost forever, so Tom Robinson went home with a heavy heart, as one can imagine. However, one of the diggers, Jimmy Bewley, a forester from Manchester who made the Lakes his home and who regularly followed and walked terriers for the Coniston Foxhounds, returned to Helm Crag and climbed down the side of the forty-foot hole. He shifted a large rock and Rags was there waiting and so the terrier was safely rescued. Jimmy Bewley was awarded a medal by the RSPCA for his efforts. It would certainly take a very tough terrier to endure such an experience.

Terriers at one time ran loose with hounds, even among the fell packs of the Lake District, but even when terriers were walked over the fells by a hunt follower, huntsman or whip, it would take a tough and hardy sort to walk anywhere up to twenty miles or so on couples and then to be asked to go to ground and bolt or kill a fox in what were more often than not vast borrans, where it took great effort for a terrier, or terriers, to pin down their fox. This was the case in 1957 after the Lunesdale Foxhounds had met in Hawes, at the Board Hotel, when they were hunting among the wild, windswept fells surrounding Hawes. Walter Parkin was huntsman then and he bred some game terrier stock descended from the famous Blencathra and Coniston terrier, Red Ike, which was bred by Albert Benson in 1932. Ike was a large terrier of sixteen inches tall, but he could get almost anywhere and proved particularly useful in deep borrans when running loose with the Blencathra Foxhounds. This knack for working deep rock holes was passed onto his progeny and Walter Parkin found this bloodline most useful in the Lunesdale country, where the very deepest of deep rock holes abound.

The Lunesdale hounds enjoyed a good hunt on the fells above Hawes that day and eventually ran their fox in at Hawes End Crag. Walter Parkin entered Rock and Tim (these may have been sons of Walter Parkin's famous Rock, which sired Breay's Ruby, the ancestor of all of today's Patterdale terriers and an incredibly game bitch), two fell terriers walked by Mister Mason of Dent, and they quickly engaged and killed the fox below ground, getting into difficulties and being unable to get out. A long dig ensued, led by that great character and terrier breeder, Frank Buck, which I think lasted for three days in all, the terriers finally being reached and pulled out, along with the dead fox, on the third day, this dig receiving quite a bit of publicity in the newspapers at the time. Many of Parkin's terriers were trapped for several days at a time in very bad places and no tougher terriers could be found anywhere.

Some earths are not only deep, but they also prove to be wet and when water isn't warmed by the sun, it is invariably at a constant icy temperature, which threatens the welfare of any terrier, no matter how game, or how tough it is. Many a tough terrier has had to be taken to the nearest farm and warmed by the fire after a long stint in a wet earth and one day during the 1960s Cyril Breay was out on the fells near his home when his terrier chased a fox into what may have been an old mine working (Casterton High Fell is littered with old drift mines, as well as mines dug for slate), or perhaps an old natural cave.

Mister Breay waited outside the earth, listening to his terrier hard at the fox for over an hour, but then the baying grew more distant until he could hear nothing. Just then two potholers appeared from around the hill and Breay told them all about his terrier chasing a fox into the rocks. One of them, attached to a rope, crawled into the opening, despite Mister Breay trying to prevent him out of fear of him getting into difficulties, but he went in anyway and the rope disappeared up to a long distance, with the potholer appearing a long time later with Breay's terrier in his arms (John Park assures me that the terrier Breay had to ground on this occasion was Rusty). The potholer told Breay that he had found the terrier in a very wet part of the earth and that he had killed the fox, but lacked the strength to get out. Breay was very grateful and returned home the three or four miles with the dog inside his coat in order to keep it warm. A warm bath and good feed later saw the terrier put to rights and this experience, kindly provided by Breay's close friend, Wally Wyld, yet again demonstrates just how tough our working terriers are.

6: THE GREYHOUND FOX:
I feel that I owe the good folk of Cumbria an apology, as I have written in the past about Greyhound Foxes in a derogatory way, proclaiming my disbelief in the existence of such a beast, but I must now eat humble pie and state that I no longer take this stance. I have changed my mind. All the research I have done over the years, and particularly recent research, into Greyhound Foxes now convinces me that this type, strain, call it what you will, of fox did indeed exist and they were, though not exactly common,

once found in most upland areas of England, Wales, Scotland and Ireland. There is just too much evidence out there supporting the existence of Greyhound Foxes, which were described in old newspaper hunting accounts as lighter coloured, larger and heavier than what was then known as the Cur Fox, referring to the lowland fox frequenting woodland, hedgerow and field, which was smaller, lighter boned and darker in colour, with much more black about the legs than their high-country cousins.

The first reference I can find for Greyhound Foxes comes rather unsurprisingly from a Cumberland newspaper which, in the 30th December 1820 issue, advertised a hunt that was to take place on Thursday January 4th 1821 when a bagged Greyhound Fox was to be released and then hounds laid on at 11am. Hunting bagged foxes was not an uncommon practice in those dim and distant days and I must strongly stress that such practices were rightfully outlawed over a century ago. This fox was to be hunted by the hounds of E. Hasell and F. Vane, but the name of the pack, or packs, isn't recorded.

A Mr John Brydon, who was a lifelong supporter of the Blencathra Foxhounds, had seen several Greyhound Foxes hunted by this famed Lakeland pack and he stated that they were bigger, stronger and 4 or 5 pounds heavier than the common red fox. Being interviewed by a reporter from the Newcastle Journal in 1950, John Brydon described just one of the many hunts he had witnessed, which occurred in 1894, with the Blencathra Foxhounds, during the first season of Jim Dalton's long and highly successful huntsmanship. He watched hounds hunt a Greyhound Fox over Latrigg at a cracking pace and saw it head up Lonscale "like greased-lightning", as he put it.

It then took hounds down the back of Skiddaw, across the beck and then away up and across the breast of the huge Blencathra Mountain. The fox eventually took them onto Blease Fell where they cast at a check, carefully working out the difficult line, till finally the fox emerged from a ravine and took off, with hounds away in full cry, following their quarry onto lower ground and across towards the Threlkeld mine-workings. Hounds fairly flew and pressed their fox hard and the master, John Crozier, in spite of his advancing years, was in time to see hounds account for what had been a fast and strong Greyhound Fox. Mister Crozier then lead the field to the Horse and Farrier Inn at Threlkeld, where he paid for the first round, a gallon of ale, which cost tenpence, with several more rounds being ordered during the celebrations. I can remember a stuffed Greyhound Fox in a glass case which was on a shelf near the fireplace of the Horse and Farrier Inn before it was renovated, and I can't help wondering if this was the fox that was caught that day. It was certainly a fox John Crozier had had mounted, as the plate stated when I read it. And I must admit, it was a big fox and it did have a lot of grey flecks in its coat, which was what caused the lighter coloured coat.

Greyhound Foxes once inhabited Dartmoor in Devonshire and one that was caught there in 1849 was massive, being five feet in length from the tip of the forepaws to the tip of the back paws, the length of the brush not included. That was a huge fox. This fact was reported in the Reading Mercury in April 1859 and the article stated this to be the largest fox ever taken. That record may well stand today. The article also stated that Greyhound Foxes were once named Wolf Foxes, due to their larger size, some of them also being noted for their large, broad heads, which gave rise to yet another name, the Bulldog Fox. It seems by the late 19th century these other names had fallen into disuse, the name Greyhound Fox being commonly used for the larger, heavier and stronger type, with its distinctive lighter coloured coat.

The North Wales Chronicle reported in November 1850 that, during the previous spring, a Greyhound Fox was caught by what is described as Mr H. R. Williams celebrated black and tan hounds (very likely the Ynysfor Hunt) on Snowdon. This hunt had a great reputation for accounting for lamb killing foxes in those days and this fox, an old toothless vixen, was at last caught after it had killed upwards of 50 lambs. A Mr W. Jones, landlord of the Dog and Pheasant Inn, Bangor, stuffed the fox, which measured 4feet 10inches in length and which stood 18inches in height.

In November 1844 the Carlisle Journal reported that Mr Crozier of the Riddings, Threlkeld, had killed a Greyhound Fox after his hounds hunted it for one hour, finally catching it at Long Close, Under Skiddaw, on Thursday October 24th 1844. Mr Cozier was a friend of the famous John Peel and his and Peel's pack enjoyed joint meets in those days. It also has to be noted that Peel's hounds hunted and sometimes caught several Greyhound Foxes, many of them in the Skiddaw and Caldbeck Fells areas.

January 23rd 1874 saw the Ullswater Hounds, hunted at that time by Abram Pattinson, known as Abe Pattinson locally, meet at Hillbeck Hall and after 'lousing' hounds Rally struck a drag, which took them to some big stones, undoubtedly one of the many Lakeland borrans favoured by foxes, where Mischief marked to ground. The huntsman put in terriers Teazer and Fury and, shortly after, a large Greyhound Fox bolted, which gave them a long hunt taking in several high fells, till it finally went to ground at Musgrave Scarth. Abe Pattinson, on reaching the spot eagerly marked by his pack, Mischief again showing the way, put in Prince and the terrier quickly seized the fox. After a struggle the huntsman was able to draw Prince and the fox, which, once Prince had very reluctantly let go his grip, was set free and hounds laid on after a little law was given. Hounds finally pulled down their fox, which was later weighed and came in at 17 pounds. Jim Watson was the Whipper-in, ably assisting Abe Pattinson.

The Cumberland Foxhounds met at Crofton Hall for their New Year's Day meet at the start of the year 1894. Hounds roused a Greyhound Fox from a chalk quarry and it made for Nether Welton; it was thought for the stronghold at Nineghylls, where hounds pressed their fox hard. Running on from Nineghylls, Reynard then made for Faulds Brow and in typical cunning fashion he crossed the line of a hare being hunted by the Abbey Holme Harriers, which resulted in both packs getting mixed up for a few minutes. The fox then headed straight for the fells, up Silver Ghyll on lofty Skiddaw and then on, now making for the huge bulk of the often mist-capped Blencathra Mountain. That fox proved to be a very game, wily customer and finally he was given best, as hounds were eventually called-off after a long, hard hunt and they then made for home.

These are just a few of many accounts of hunts that featured Greyhound Foxes, the evidence being overwhelming that such a beast once existed in many upland areas. Such accounts are the main reason, together with the testimony of many very experienced foxhunters, that I have changed my mind on this subject. I am now a firm believer in the Greyhound Fox and its speed, strength and tenacity that made this strain of fox a legend.

7: THE WORKING TECKEL – HOUND OR TERRIER?:

The working teckel is a game little dog that has been, and still is, used for a variety of different tasks, but it is also a dog breed which possesses both hound qualities and qualities more akin to a working terrier. However, the answer to the question featured in the above title is, I believe, very easy to conclude, as the teckel is undoubtedly a working hound, rather than a working terrier. Seeing them at work is what provides such a conclusion.

Although I have never owned a working teckel, I have hunted a mixed pack of teckels and terriers alongside John Hill and I have to say that I found them to be very useful little working hounds, having also hunted with Chipper Smith's working teckels. Before the hunting ban John and I hunted rabbit, hare and fox with our mixed pack and my terriers learnt much from the teckels when it came to casting at a check and sticking to a line, rather than over-running in their eagerness to push on after quarry, which meant that they vastly improved when it came to work above ground. This is because teckels work in every way like a hound.

Terriers can certainly hunt well above ground, but when not worked alongside hounds they generally do not stick to a line for too long, being too impatient and eager to push on, to keep casting themselves at a bad check. I have hunted many hundreds of foxes above ground with my small terrier pack before they hunted alongside teckels, but they never stuck to a line for too long. After working alongside John Hill's teckels, hunts of forty minutes or more were not uncommon, which is quite a feat for a terrier. True, terriers, when it was safe and legal to run them loose with a pack, have often been seen leading hounds, at least for a time (a keen Blencathra Foxhounds follower told of a time when he was working out on the fells and one of Johnny Richardson's terriers came flying past on the scent of a fox, quickly followed by the Blencathra pack), but that is because hunt terriers of those days learnt from the hounds they ran with.

I found teckels to be very busy, eager little hunting hounds that can push on through dense undergrowth at quite a pace, flushing many rabbits and hunting their line keenly. They hunted hares with equal enthusiasm and could stick to a line, casting themselves in a wide circle at a bad check and often getting the hunt away again. And at fox they were as keen as mustard, with some teckels even going to ground in the manner of a working terrier. John's Fatima, a tiny mite of a teckel bred by Nick Valentine, was one such teckel which readily went to ground and one day, while the rest of the pack went away hunting a rabbit they had flushed, Fatima got into a dug-out rabbit hole and began baying eagerly at a fox. Fell went in and killed the fox, but Fatima worked very well, baying eagerly while avoiding getting bitten, in much the same manner as a traditional Jack Russell terrier will work.

There are several teckel packs up and down the country and others cross teckels with beagles in order to produce a small working basset type hound and some of these are incredibly good workers. The grandfather of my own dog, Bracken, was a teckel/beagle cross and he was superb at work. Bud was owned and worked by Chipper Smith and was used at rabbit, rat and fox, flushing foxes to waiting guns, and his cry was something to be heard. I saw Bud at work on these fox drives and was most impressed with his abilities, as well as Chipper's excellent hound control.

Some breeders cross teckels with terriers too and some of these are also excellent workers. In fact, if you are having problems with fine bone and lack of good nose in your terrier strain, then an outcross to a working teckel would undoubtedly correct such faults, as long as you do not show. The resultant offspring would certainly be unsuitable for showing, but they would make cracking workers and those who work terriers within the law needn't worry about such a cross weakening that terrier instinct for going to ground. Simply use a teckel stud dog that readily goes to ground, as many do. It is true that some teckels will not go to ground, but then some terriers are the same and there are some terriers that will go to ground, but they will not work large quarry, so I wouldn't worry about that. A teckel outcross would do no harm to terrier instinct, but it would vastly improve finding ability and good bone would also result, not to mention a strong bay when working either above or below ground. I believe a teckel/border terrier cross would be most useful, as border terriers are descended from small, long-bodied dogs that gave rise to Dandie-Dinmont terriers from which border terriers have been bred, together with other breeds such as small bull terriers once common in the north, fell terriers and Irish terriers.

The only drawback I could see to having teckels in the area John and I hunted was that they struggled a bit over rough ground and they were affected at times by severely cold and damp weather when subjected to a long day on the moors. I think a teckel/terrier or teckel/beagle cross is more suited to hunting high moorland, but for hunting lowland areas one would find it hard to better a pack of hard working teckels. They have superb noses, good drive and plenty of voice, though their cry is not as glorious as that of beagles or working basset hounds. Teckels have such good noses that many stalkers now use them for tracking wounded deer. Teckels are simply superb small working hounds and having hunted with them many, many times I can highly recommend them to those trying to decide which breed of working dog they will keep.

8: WORKING TERRIER HEALTH-TRIED & TESTED TREATMENTS:
The basic requirements for keeping working terriers in good health is obviously to provide a warm, dry and draught-free bed, good food in the proper quantities and a sufficient amount of clean, fresh water daily. Add to this plenty of regular exercise and appropriate discipline and socialising and working terriers will thrive, giving their owners years of hard work. But there is more to keeping terriers in fine fettle than these few obvious basics, such as good and diligent practices when it comes to treating bites and other injuries, such as thorns in pads, which can cause a great deal of suffering to any terrier unfortunate enough to have a thorn penetrate its

flesh. This puts me in mind of one of the best huntsmen the Lake District has produced – Joe Wear, who hunted the Ullswater Foxhounds for many years.

Eddie Pool of Patterdale reveres the memory of this huntsman and one day he told me of how Joe, after finishing hunting and arriving back in kennels, would check every hound for thorns stuck in pads or skin, treating any injuries immediately and then seeing to his game stock of terriers in a similar manner, treating bites promptly. A terrier with a thorn in its pad will be lame, even reluctant to put its paw on the ground, so a thorough check over is essential and then the thorn can usually be pulled out using a sterilised pin and tweezers. Occasionally though, the end of a thorn can be left deeply embedded in the pad and in such cases it is probably better for the vet to take a look and treat the injury. Once the thorn is extracted, dipping and soaking the paw in salt water four times a day will extract any badness in the fight against infection. Salt water is one of the most effective ways of drawing out infected material from a wound and I use this same treatment on any cuts or bites four times a day. This is a most effective way of keeping wounds clean and I have found that the salt content also dries-up the wound very quickly too. Do not use creams on wounds, as they keep them moist and thus more prone to infection. If you can get your hands on anti-biotic powder, then sprinkle the wound or bite with this a few minutes after bathing with salt water and this too will help dry-up and keep the wound clean. Depending on the severity of the bite or injury, bathing with salt water should continue for between three and five days, or a little longer in some cases. Antibiotics should be given only in more serious cases, and according to veterinary advice, as younger terriers in particular will fight off infection pretty quickly without them. Alternatively, Hibbiscrub is also very good for cleaning wounds and one cannot beat TCP for treating bee or wasp stings.

The eyes are always worth checking after a day in the field, especially when terriers have been bushing in undergrowth or when they have been to ground. Small seeds can get into the eyes from disturbed undergrowth and if left can cause problems. Worse still, after a session to ground, especially after a dig, soil and grit, or even sand, can get into the eyes and this needs washing out as soon as possible. It is worth keeping an eye wash in the car, or even in a bag on your person, so that eyes can be washed out immediately. Good eye washes can be purchased from any chemist shop and they are most effective, though boiled water allowed to cool in a sterilised container is also suitable for the task of washing much debris out of the eyes. Just simply pour gently onto the eyes and wipe with cotton wool pads. I find that my wife's make-up remover pads are ideal for this, not to mention for cleaning out bites and wounds too.

I have seen my terriers in some filthy states after a dig, especially after being in soft soil or peat earths, so I always give them a good warm bath when I get them home, making certain that no soapy water gets anywhere near the eyes and ears. Give them a good rub down with a suitably dry towel to make certain they are as dry as possible and then get some warm food inside them. There is nothing like a warm meal for boosting a terrier's strength after a long stint to ground at fox (Do your best to carry out terrier work within the law of the country in which you hunt), placing them under heat lamps when necessary (if kennelled, otherwise a warm fireside will do), for maybe a couple of days, just till they regain energy. The late, great Cyril Breay always gave his terriers a warm bath after a hard stint to ground at large quarry and undoubtedly he gave them a warm meal afterwards too. Breay's kennel management skills, in fact, were second-to-none and the welfare of his charges was always a priority, as it should be with any good terrierman.

When a terrier suffers from diarrhoea or vomiting it is important to replace body fluids in order to avoid dehydration. Cut out solid foods and milk at such times (I don't give adult dogs milk anyway) and keep getting fluids into your terrier using boiled water left to cool, mixed with glucose, giving a couple of teaspoonfuls regularly throughout the day. For diarrhoea, a mixture of boiled water and arrowroot is effective, when given three times a day. Sachets of arrowroot can be purchased from any decent supermarket and I usually give a full sachet at a time. Milk of Magnesia is excellent for stopping vomiting and a teaspoonful every three hours will usually sort the matter out. Cut out food for forty-eight hours, making certain you provide plenty of fluids already discussed, but if symptoms persist beyond two or three days, then a visit to the vets might be necessary. If your terrier is vomiting and it has diarrhoea too, being unable to keep anything down, drinking lots of water, but vomiting it back up, then gastro enteritis is probably the cause and veterinary treatment will be essential.

Another way to help your working terriers to enjoy good health and vitality is simply to allow them regular access to grass. Grass works in three different ways for dogs and they seem able to control how they use it. Firstly, they will eat grass and then vomit in order to get rid of anything lying on their stomach that won't digest. Secondly, they will eat grass and retain it, using it as an aid to digestion. And, thirdly, they will eat grass and pass it through their system very quickly, within minutes usually, before defecating. This cleans out their intestines and bowel. Plain and simple grass is very effective in maintaining good health in dogs. We do well to look after our working terriers diligently, for then they will reward us with faithful service for many seasons to come.

9: TURK – MEMORIES OF A GREAT WORKING TERRIER:

I have been blessed with a number of great working terriers over the years and one of the best among them was Turk, which I bred myself out of Fell and Mist. Turk was certainly well-bred and he was part of a litter that produced consistently good workers. Neil Wilson's very game Alfie, my own bitch Beck and Carl Noon's Flint were Turk's litter brothers and sister and the whole bunch proved extremely useful. Turk, in fact, was extremely game, though I did have my doubts about him when he was a puppy. He was the only one in the litter that was a little on the shy and nervous side and while the rest rushed out into the garden to play, Turk would cautiously approach the open doorway and look out nervously, almost afraid to step outside. I wondered then about his future – whether or not he would prove suitable for working large quarry such as foxes.

Fell was bred by Wendy Pinkney of Wensleydale Foxhounds fame and he was bred from some of the best working bloodlines in the country, including Harry Hardisty's Turk, Cowen's Rock, Graham Ward, Middleton and Breay and Buck lines too. Mist was bred along similar lines, but carried far more lines back to Breay and Buck stock. Both of these terriers proved very game and useful above and below ground and they shared a number of ancestors in common, being distantly-related, so I decided to breed from them and Turk was just one of their offspring. He entered to his first holed-fox at a dug-out rabbit hole on the edge of a steep wooded valley near Rochdale, getting to ground behind his dam, Mist, and quickly bolting a fox, which the whole pack of terriers then hunted down through the wood and to the other side of the valley, eventually losing its line on a steep hillside covered in shale – spoil left over from the mining era which once thrived in this district. It was a thrill to see Turk eagerly get to ground, share in bolting the fox, as his bay clearly signalled, and then hunt it with the terriers baying and yapping as they followed the hot scent for as long as possible. Turk never looked back after that, though, as he progressed, I noticed that he never lost that cautious, almost nervous approach to an uncertain situation, but I need never have worried as to his future working ability, which proved to be exceptional.

That caution enabled Turk to work foxes, even game and hardy hill foxes, with much sense and he never once suffered a mauling from a fox. Shortly after that first encounter with fox below ground (Turk had shared in bushing several foxes before beginning earth work) Turk once more went to earth, but Mist got in ahead of him and she was first up to her fox in quite a tight spot. In such a situation a terrier behind the first can often cause problems, as the lead terrier cannot dodge the lunges of the fox and will often take a severe mauling, so I was a little worried, but that cautious, sensible attitude meant that I needn't have worried at all, as Turk simply emerged after a few moments, looking for another way in to his fox. Mist was then able to work unhindered and bolted what turned out to be a large dog fox, then going on to settle with another. A hard dig ensued and the following day Mist and a dead vixen were finally reached. It is always best to work terriers alone, though I have always bushed with mine and so terriers getting to ground together has often resulted when they have come upon a fox to ground among briars or gorse. Thankfully, my terriers generally have had the sense to emerge in search of another route to their quarry and so severe maulings because of a terrier blocking the rear has rarely been a problem, excepting a few occasions.

One of Turk's best days was when he came in very handy at a difficult earth where his sire, Fell, was having problems with a large fox. This was at a two-holed earth. Fell was in alone and working his quarry well, but it settled in a very commanding position between two very dense tree roots at the base of the large tree. I dug down, which was far from easy going, finally breaking through above where fell was working, his head in among the roots as he tried to better his opponent. However, that large fox was punishing him every time he attempted to draw it, his quarry being larger and heavier than he was, so he wasn't really getting anywhere. However, Turk was fifteen inches tall and a good nineteen pounds in weight in his prime and he was also very agile and very strong. In spite of his size he could get himself into some very tight places and he could weave his way through a rockpile with seemingly no effort. That agility now served him well. After more than a little struggle, I was able to grab Fell and pull him out of the earth, immediately replacing him with Turk, who entered at the hole I had dug, which made it a little more difficult, as he had to negotiate the steep angle and then twist himself into the tree roots. A few bays later and now seeing his chance, he grabbed the large and heavy fox and actually drew it from what was a very good vantage and stronghold. I honestly thought that fox would best any terrier sent to try it, but Turk's extra size, weight and strength enabled him to draw that fox from one of the most secure earths a fox could have chosen. That day I realised that this terrier was something a bit special.

This was confirmed on a number of occasions, such as the day towards the end of the season when Turk marked and entered a dug-out rabbit hole on the edge of the West Pennines near Ramsbottom and promptly bolted a dog fox, before grabbing and drawing the vixen out of the earth. On another occasion, in the same general area, Turk once again got to ground and a hard dig eventually uncovered a very dead vixen. Turk had two bites around his mouth, as he avoided the jaw to jaw encounter and killed his foxes by grabbing them by the throat, turning them over on their back and throttling them, which is the most humane and least damaging way a harder terrier can work.

I have always attempted to work within the confines of the Hunting Act 2004, but inevitably terriers of the quality of Turk will get to ground on foxes, even when they are used for bushing rabbits, but very often my terriers have got to ground in areas that are also shoots, so terrier work to earth has been legal anyway, it is just that some terriers will kill foxes that do not bolt quickly and that is unavoidable. The important thing is to keep working our terriers, doing our best to keep within the law and utilizing exemptions when necessary.

Sadly, poor Turk's health deteriorated and I had to have him put down, though he had enjoyed a great "innings" of fifteen and a-half years, with thirteen seasons and over three-hundred foxes to his credit.

10: HISTORIC LAMBING CALLS WITH THE LAKELAND FELL PACKS:

One of the most important functions for the Lakeland Fell Packs was to be on call during springtime to deal with any foxes which took to worrying lambs. They would purposely finish their fixtures at the end of March or even into April, so as to be on hand should any farmers telephone to report lamb losses, which losses were sometimes heavy. Historic hunting reports are full of springtime lambing, or lamb worrying calls, but sadly since the Hunting Act of 2004, which came into force in February 2005, farmers cannot turn to the fell packs in an effort to protect their livelihoods from marauding foxes, which, after all, are efficient and ruthless predators that often prey on lambs (two hounds can legally be used to flush foxes to guns). I can remember Tommy Graves, lifelong supporter of the Coniston Foxhounds and a great help to the various huntsmen from Anthony Chapman's time omwards, telling me about a fox that took nine lambs over three nights from pastures under Loughrigg Fell and of how Anthony Chapman responded to the farmer calling him in, successfully catching the lamb killer and putting an immediate end to the losses with his fabulous Coniston Foxhounds.

It beggars-belief that a farmer cannot call a pack of hounds in to protect his livelihood, the law putting the rights of foxes, recognized agricultural pests, ahead of those who try to make a living from land and livestock. When Anthony Barker hunted the Ullswater Foxhounds from 1941 to 1946 while Joe Wear was serving in the armed forces during World War 2, he was often called out to deal with lamb worrying foxes and sometimes he was out hunting 7 or 8 days a week in order to fit in all the farmers who were experiencing problems. The Forest Hall Farm had called hounds in and Anthony took hounds and terriers there in his windowless car, which was used to transport hounds during the war, staying overnight and getting a very early start, 'lousing' his hounds at daybreak.

The lamb killer proved to be a vixen with cubs and the terriers marked an earth under some stones after hounds had hunted from about here, with the cubs being accounted for and the vixen caught by hounds after quite a long hunt at 7am, going after the dog fox the very next morning, this fox eventually being caught by Trilby in a peat hag, which put a swift end to the lamb losses at Forest Hall. Just after this he was called out to a farm at Grasmere and he walked his hounds over the fells and stayed the night there. He then spent the next two days hunting lamb killing foxes and hounds caught two. He then had to take hounds to Hartsop Hall close to the foot of the Kirkstone Fells and there hounds marked a fox in, which Anthony accounted for with the terriers. These are just a few of many lamb worrying calls Anthony Barker answered during his very successful years as huntsman of the Ullswater Pack, which very aptly demonstrated the value of a pack of hounds when it comes to protecting livestock and thus the farmers livelihoods. Three of the terriers used by Barker during the war years were Rock, Whin and Fleming's Myrt. Rock was a great fox killer and was regularly used when a lamb killing fox was to ground. He was on loan to Anthony Barker, owned by Joe Wilkinson, who gave up his post whipping-in at the Ullswater to return to farming during the war. Rock returned to Joe's South Lakeland farm when he retired and once there killed every cat on the premises.

Anthony Chapman and his Coniston hounds and terriers answered many lamb-worrying calls over the years and just one of these was in the mid-1960s when there were many problems at various farms through April and May. May 1st saw Anthony drawing the lambing fields at 5am at Satterthwaite. Hounds struck a drag and stuck to it right into the forestry, rousing the lamb killer and hunting it to Dale Park, where it gave the pack a hard time for about an hour or so, before going away and a very long hunt followed until he finally went to ground below Brock Crag, back at Dale Park. Tess was put in and bolted the fox, which was hunted for a few minutes before going to ground again. Jess and Rags were put in and they killed the fox, a big dog fox, after a five- hour hunt in all. Jess belonged to Keith Clement of Kendal and she was a black terrier descended from Cyril Breay's Flint line, Flint probably being a son of Breay's Gem, or possibly her brother.

The final lambing call of that season was at Stool End Farm, Langdale and a fox was hunted around Crinkle Crags and finally killed under Kettle Crags, thus ending that spring's run of lamb worrying calls that had resulted in at least eleven lamb killing foxes being accounted for. One cannot put a price on such a valuable way of protecting farm livestock and livelihoods from the very damaging predations of an agricultural pest. I say very damaging because a fox will often continue to kill lambs at the same farm if it isn't caught quickly. Such was the case one spring at Hartsop Hall when a fox killed 19 lambs over several nights. Hounds hunted the fox for several days in a row without success, till on the fifth attempt he was finally caught by the Ullswater Pack.

11: ORIGINS OF MISTER BREAY'S STRAIN:

It is unknown exactly when Cyril Breay began working terriers, but one thing we do know is that, before 1920, and probably for a number of years up to that time, including the time when he was first married, at St Mary's Church, Windermere in August 1918, he was working a strain of Sealyham terrier that Breay himself stated had its origins in South Wales. The Sealyham terrier of those days was a game worker of fox, badger and otter and there were several working strains up and down the country. Which strain was kept by Breay is again unknown, but he gives us a clue when he stated that South Wales was where his working terrier strain originated from, referring of course to the Sealyham influence that went into his fell terrier breeding programme that he began in 1920.

My research recently led me to an old newspaper article from 1915 that tells of how Lord Lonsdale kept a strain of Sealyham terrier that he used for badger and fox digging on his vast estate (the gentry of the Lake District of those days all kept their own strains of terrier, bred by their gamekeepers or specially employed kennelmen, which were used very often at organised badger digs, with otterhounds during the summer and for fox control on their estates during winter, though several of these terriers were on loan to the various fell packs, as Lord Lonsdale also kept a strain of fell terrier which supposedly had existed since 1720). This strain was famous for its courage and Lord Lonsdale went on to tell the reporter that he obtained foundation terriers for his Sealyham terrier strain from Haverford West in South Wales. Could it be that Cyril Breay obtained his Sealyham terriers from Lord Lonsdale, or more than likely from Lord Lonsdale's gamekeepers, as Cyril Breay certainly knew many northern gamekeepers and assisted them with fox control throughout his lifetime, including gamekeepers on the Lowther Estate, some of whom later kept terriers from Breay's increasingly sought-after strain of fell terrier? I think it highly likely.

Mister Breay hunted a lot of low country in those days, but when his interest in fell hunting moved him to follow the fell packs he found that his Sealyham terriers, being rather short legged, struggled to cross rough ground that abounds in North Yorkshire, Westmorland and Cumberland; the areas where he spent much of his hunting life. Sealyham terriers were fine for digging badgers, foxes and for bolting otters in places like the Lune Valley, where Breay often worked his terriers, but the rough fell country and deep rock earths and old mine workings of the high country were a totally different matter and heavily boned, short legged types really struggled to keep up across the fells and moors. They found it even more difficult to negotiate some of the earths commonly frequented by foxes, especially foxes that are hard pressed and which deliberately headed for what they knew to be safer strongholds. And so, Mister Breay, greatly impressed with the Sealyham as a worker, sought outcross blood and no gamer outcross blood could be found than that of the local fell terrier strains that had been tested in some of the deepest and most difficult places in the country, without being found wanting.

Cyril Breay married his first wife at St Mary's Church, Windermere in August 1918 when he lived somewhere in the area, possibly at Kendal. Research and testimony from Cyril Breay's son, Robin, suggests that he hunted with the Coniston Foxhounds at that time, and probably the Ullswater too, which pack regularly hunted on the outskirts of Kendal in those days, so he had access to some superb fell terrier bloodlines with which to begin his strain, choosing in the end a Coniston terrier which he put over one or more of his Sealyham bitches. John Park told me it was

Coniston Jummy that Breay used, as by 1920 Jummy had earned a reputation as an incredible worker and could work foxes out of some of the deepest borrans in the Coniston country, including the infamous Broad-Howe Borran, but this is by no means certain. Another contender is Anthony Chapman's Crab, which was then a famous fox killer and one which successfully worked foxes even in such death-trap places as the old "rubbish" heaps at Kirkstone Quarries, which were huge piles of rocks rejected by the quarrymen (Anthony Chapman was the father of George Chapman, huntsman at that time of the Coniston Foxhounds). Coniston Crag was another superb worker at this time and a great fox killer. Whatever the terrier used, it had to be a great finder and one that could kill a fox below ground single-handed, as Breay would settle for nothing less – hence the reason he produced terriers, generation after generation, that earned reputations as great finders and fox killers (though many of Breay's terriers were great fox bolters, as he bolted foxes and shot them when controlling foxes for gamekeepers).

Mister Breay put in more outcross blood in the 1930s, using a Border terrier stud he purchased from a Mister Robson of Carlisle, the hardest terrier Breay ever saw at work, and a little later he put in white fell terrier blood from Jack Porter's Eskdale and Ennerdale Metz, after Breay watched him bolt three foxes from Shiningstones earth near Sedbergh, which had a reputation as a place from which foxes couldn't be bolted. Mister Breay then stuck to his linebreeding programme and produced terriers with some obvious bull and Scottish terrier influence that later became known as Patterdale terriers, this name first being used for Breay and Buck bred terriers by terriermen of the Rossendale Valley in Lancashire, which included a young and incredibly enthusiastic Brian Nuttall.

Mister Breay's strain of working terrier, be they fell or Patterdale terriers, has had a massive influence on modern strains of working terrier and little by little we are discovering the origins of these popular bloodlines, though I still cannot help feeling that we have just scratched the surface.

12: CARING FOR THE MENTAL WELFARE OF OUR WORKING DOGS:

Working breeds of dog have been bred to be alert and very active and such breeding can, during periods of little activity in particular, result in problems which mostly stem from a lack of mental stimulation, though a lack of physical activity can also result in behavioural problems such as constant barking, especially when working dogs are kennelled. A lot of hunting folk keep their working dogs in the family home and a constantly barking dog, or worse still, a number of constantly barking dogs, may result in complaints from neighbours that in turn results in strained relations at best, and possible eviction at worst, where property is rented. So what can we do in order to keep our working dogs mentally stimulated during periods of non-work, such as during the summer off-season?

Exercise is obviously a key factor in physically tiring working dogs when not actually working, but exercise alone doesn't always mentally stimulate dogs to a satisfactory degree and I currently own a beagle cross that has enjoyed long walks ever since being vaccinated, but this does not prevent her from being problematic when not gainfully employed, so I have to use other methods to help keep her mentally stimulated. When working dogs are content they will spend much of their time sleeping and they will be generally well behaved. When not content, working dogs can chew, bark, howl and generally get up to no good. They may even become aggressive with other dogs. A good routine of exercise remains essential, but there are other things that can be done to improve behaviour.

An excellent way of mentally stimulating bored dogs is to enhance and enrich their feeding routine with puzzle and other enrichment feeders, which is a method I have had to employ with my beagle cross and her behaviour has improved dramatically as a result. I feed her in three parts. Firstly, she has some food from a bowl alongside my other dogs and then she has more food stuffed inside a tough rubber cylinder known as a Kong. It takes great effort for a dog to get all the food out of this feeder and that tires them both mentally and physically. And finally she has the rest of her food in a puzzle feeder – a ball she pushes around in order to shake the food out of it in dribs and drabs. Her feeding time has gone from about a minute or a little more, to over half-an-hour and she has to put a lot of effort into getting at her food, which results in a more content and restful dog. I feed her in this manner even after she has had a long working day and she then settles for the night very well indeed.

My beagle cross is still full of mischief, having a very strong personality, but her behaviour is now much better. It is important to tackle behavioural problems because these usually betray that a dog is not content (some dogs behave badly because of being cruelly treated either as a puppy, or by a former owner). Not only that, but bad behaviour can spread among the other dogs and so it is vital to stamp it out as quickly as possible.

Some may think that feeding with puzzle feeders and other devices that make it essential that a dog puts both physical and mental effort into obtaining its food is a waste of time, but all one is doing is providing a more natural way of feeding. I was in professional hunt service for several years and keeping hounds happy is not easy. We walked them out and let them play and stretch their legs in the grass-yard. They obviously work during the season when they are at their most content, but there are times when they are more or less confined to kennels, when the bitches are in season as an example, and so they can become bored. However, we fed mostly raw flesh and it takes great effort, both physically and mentally, for hounds to feed on a carcass. They rip and tear and get into every nook and cranny for every morsel they can get at and this takes both time and a great deal of effort. Our hounds are always happiest after feeding on flesh, stripping a carcass in the process. It takes little effort for them to feed on meal from a trough and so feeding flesh is always the best option when possible.

When it comes to domestic working dogs, either kept in the home or in kennel, using puzzle feeders and devices like the Kong, or even hard bones (never feed cooked bones, as these can splinter and cause lethal internal injuries) stuffed with food, is imitating this natural method and this can only be good for a dog, working or otherwise. I cannot stress enough however, that feeding in this manner is no substitute for regular periods of exercise. Feeding with enrichment feeders compliments other methods of keeping our working breeds happy and thus content.

Another way of keeping dogs happy and stimulated is with the use of bones, or substitute bones. A good hard knuckle bone will keep dogs occupied for a great deal of time and will tire your dog mentally and physically as it works out ways to get at whatever morsels it can. Cow-hide bones are another option, though I do not use these as they end up a sticky, wet, horrible mass of pulp in the end. I have found such things as nyla-bones better, as these are very tough and they do not splinter. They break-up very slowly in tiny pieces which simply pass through dogs that chew them. These are great for providing the more energetic dogs with something to do when they are stuck at home, or in kennel, while you are at work (never leave two or more dogs alone together with bones, as fights will undoubtedly result).

Animal care has moved on in leaps and bounds since I first started hunting in the 1970s and it is important that we do our best to keep up. True, some go way over the top when it comes to their dogs, often treating them better than they treat people or treating them like little children, which is ridiculous, but it is vital to give our working dogs proper care and to employ various methods to keep them happy and content to whatever degree is necessary. These are just a few ideas and I hope they may be helpful, as they have proven helpful in my own household.

13: FRANK BUCK – A ONE-MAN WORKING TERRIER RESCUE SYSTEM:

Frank Buck of Harmby, near Leyburn in Wensleydale, must be ranked as one of the greatest terriermen this country has ever produced and, although Frank sadly passed away during the early 1990s, the influence of his strain remains massive among various types of working terrier. I come from an area sandwiched between the South and West Pennines and throughout the whole of this region Frank Buck's breeding was used by most terriermen and so I became familiar with his strain from my early teens onwards. Of course, when I say Frank Buck's breeding, I also include the breeding of Cyril Breay's strain, as the two were and still are inextricably linked, though it is also true to say that Frank Buck bred and sold stock in much greater numbers than did Cyril Breay, who was more than a little hesitant about letting folk he didn't know and trust have his bloodlines.

Frank Buck was a very outgoing character and he bred and sold puppies in large numbers, which means that terriers from his strain are now found up and down the country. Not only was Buck a very skilled breeder of working terriers, many of which were lookers too, but he also had a great knack for rescuing trapped terriers and many would call on his services when terriers were in trouble. The fellpacks of Lakeland and North Yorkshire certainly called him out on a number of occasions, but possibly his most important rescue occurred in 1936 at Bishopdale, after two of Cyril Breay's earth dogs got into trouble, becoming trapped in a difficult rock earth. I know I have written about this rescue before, when Breay was introduced to Frank Buck by Walter Parkin, who then whipped-in at the Lunesdale Hunt, serving under the huntsmanship of Tommy Robinson and often hunting hounds for Tommy, but John Park, a close friend of both Buck and Breay and a superb terrierman in his own right, has recently provided much more information told to him by Mister Breay himself and so I thought it well worth sharing.

Mister Breay could see the two terriers down among the rocks far below inside this bad earth, but neither himself nor others present, such as Walter Parkin, could do anything to get them out. Mister Breay was on the verge of throwing meat laced with strychnine down to the pair in order to put them out of their misery (at the time strychnine poisoning was considered to be a painless death and this poison was occasionally used to end the suffering of terriers hopelessly trapped to ground), but Walter Parkin convinced him to wait, as he knew a chap who might be able to help. And then the historic and important meeting of Breay and Buck followed, with Frank bringing along some quarrymen, an expert dynamiter among them.

Mister Breay was told that if dynamite was used it would kill the terriers, but Frank Buck persuaded the expert to try to figure out some way of breaking the massive rock impeding the rescue. He later told Frank Buck to drill into each side of the rock and place the dynamite inside. This was done and Frank succeeded in cracking the huge rock in two, the pieces then rolling down the fellside. The terriers could then be got out and it was probably with the use of meat on the end of a rope that the terriers would grab and hold onto while hauled out (a common method of rescuing terriers in the Lakes and Dales of Yorkshire where deep rock earths abound). This rescue cemented an unlikely friendship between two completely opposite characters that went on to produce a race of terrier that is second to none when it comes to earth work.

Buck was called out numerous times by the Lunesdale Foxhounds under both Walter Parkin and John Nicholson, Parkin's whip and successor, with some rescues lasting for several days. One rescue at Hawes End Crag lasted for three days and two terriers were safely got out. Another successful rescue was at Coverdale, a valley that has produced some of the greatest racing stables for the last two-hundred years at least. And yet another rescue involved two of Buck's own terriers, Tex and Chew, which again lasted for a few days, with both terriers eventually being got out safely, after a thirty-foot dig into this rocky stronghold at a crag on Addleborough, the flat-topped fell which often appeared in the TV series *All Creatures Great and Small*.

Mister Breay also called on Frank Buck on other occasions when he had terriers trapped to ground, but, in spite of Buck's expertise at rescuing trapped terriers, often with the necessary use of dynamite, Breay still lost about eleven terriers during a lifetime of working some of the most dangerous ground in the country, where many limestone earths lead into the ground for literally miles in some cases. Potholing in these areas was popular in Breay's time and indeed potholers helped rescue Rusty on at least one occasion.

Frank Buck was responsible for the rescue of many working terriers, several of his own among them, which can no doubt be counted in dozens. He received medals from the RSPCA for his efforts and this truly ebullient character didn't shy away from the limelight, or the attention his efforts brought him. It is sad that such men have to grow old and die, for the fells are no longer producing such characters and the working terrier world is surely a poorer place without the expertise and drive of such a character as the great Frank Buck.

14: WEATHERPROOF WORKING TERRIERS:

A little earlier I wrote about the need to be careful about when and where you put a terrier to ground due to climatic changes, particularly increasing bouts of storms and heavy rain, so it seems reasonable to discuss the various coat types of our working terriers and which type is most desirable. Like entering methods, coat type is a controversial subject that will undoubtedly continue to be debated long into the future, as opinion differs greatly with regard to this subject.

Some prefer a smooth coat and their reasons for doing so are somewhat persuasive. When interviewed by Brian Plummer, John Nicholson, the long-serving late huntsman of the Lunesdale Foxhounds which hunt some of the most exposed and windswept country imaginable, stated that he had seen Cyril Breay's terriers out with hounds on many occasions and that they were at their best when working deep earths in freezing conditions, but the truth is that, while some of Mister Breay's terriers were indeed smooth coated, many were also broken coated. The smooth coated terriers of Breay and Buck's famous strain, which is far more popular now than when these two great terriermen were still alive and very active when it came to terrier work, had what is known in Lakeland as 'slape' coats, 'slape' being a sort of Lake District slang for 'slippery,' which denotes smooth, but such jackets were incredibly tight-knit and very dense, rather than being the sort of smooth coat found on some Jack Russells today, for instance, which are really quite fine. These smooth, or 'slape' coats were thus very resistant to rain and wind.

I have interviewed many excellent and experienced terriermen over several decades and one thing they tend to agree on is that cold wind and persistent rain presents the greatest danger to a working terrier, particularly one that was compelled to wait outside an earth while another terrier was to ground. Many argue that a smooth coated terrier can quickly shake water from its coat and there is something in what they say. However, a terrier with a very tight, hard and wiry jacket will also quickly shake the water from its coat. In doing so, many a terrier has saved itself from freezing to death on an exposed hill, moor or fell.

One thing I will say for smooth coated terriers is that their coat is far more easily cleaned, especially after a stint to ground. A terrier with a hard wiry jacket will not get too badly 'clagged' up with soil or peat, but one with a long open coat will soon be amply covered, making cleaning a nightmare. Long open coats are not desirable on a working terrier, especially when the weather is bitterly cold, though occasionally a terrier is bred that defies such reasoning. My own terrier Turk had such a coat and, while his jacket did get clagged up quite badly during encounters with fox below ground, I have never seen him suffer in any way from the cold and I have hunted very exposed moorland and fell for decades. I have seen my terriers shivering with cold at times when pegged down near an earth being worked by another terrier, but I never once saw Turk doing so. He seemed impervious to cold and wet, in spite of a very poor jacket. The rest of the litter Turk was born into all had excellent jackets, but his was incredibly poor, having thrown-back to the old Bedlington influence which saturated early fell and Lakeland terrier breeding during the days before the Great War (1914-1918).

I personally prefer a 'slape' coat to a traditional smooth coat which is more akin to a bull terrier than a terrier required to work in often freezing conditions, as 'slape' coated terriers have plenty of density. In fact, I believe such a coat is the best for keeping out wind and rain, though one with a hard, wiry jacket similar to coconut matting is also very weatherproof (Sid Wilkinson's Rock had such a jacket, as did his sire, Anthony Barker's Rock). I avoid terriers with a smooth coat similar to that of a bull terrier and I also mostly avoid terriers with long open coats, in spite of the fact that I have owned two such terriers over the years, Turk and Bella, a daughter of Rock.

When one considers some of the earths worked by our terriers, it is easy to understand why good coat is important. The late Joe Armstrong of Dalston in Cumbria, a truly great terrierman in his day with a wealth of experience at hunting large quarry and one who hunted with the great Willie Irving of Melbreak Foxhounds fame, once had a terrier to ground in a freezing drainage pipe half filled with water for thirty hours. Upon emerging, Armstrong remarked that his terrier's coat, one bred out of Irving stock, crackled with ice when he touched it. A terrier must have plenty of density and natural oils in its coat in order to survive such harsh conditions whilst at work. My own terriers have been trapped in rockpiles on a few occasions during midwinter and early spring, when the weather can often be at its worst, and they have been forced to survive very cold temperatures overnight. In fact, when Rock was trapped in a large rockpile in late April 1987, snow fell and a hard frost set in over the two days she was to ground, yet she seemed none the worse for her ordeal. In fact, she would have happily returned to ground had I allowed her to do so.

Scores of experiences demonstrate that a terrier needs a good coat if it is to survive, even thrive, on regular hard work in often hostile conditions, yet opinion continues to differ as to which type is best. I suppose the best type of jacket is the type which suits best each individual terrierman's needs. Experience teaches one many things and that is true of coat type. Whatever the type, a weatherproof jacket with natural oils and density is essential, especially nowadays when wind and rain seems to be ever more frequent.

15: THE WORKING TERRIER PUPPY – HOUSE TRAINING TIPS:

Working terrier puppies, or puppies of any working breed come to that, bring a lot of fun and happiness into the family home, but it is also true to say that not every aspect of having a puppy is pleasant. Especially is this true when it comes to house training. The principles of house training puppies are very simple, but not all puppies respond in the same way.

For instance, in my experience at least, I have found that dog puppies generally respond more quickly to house training than do bitch puppies. It is not easy to understand why this is so, but I believe it is simply because dogs are instinctively territorial and are thus more aware of their environment than bitches. Dog puppies will very often quickly catch on that soiling their immediate environment is not acceptable and thus they are clean sometimes after only a few days of training. I think this has been true of all my dog puppies, but it has been very different with bitch puppies, which, in some cases, tend to take several weeks (sometimes months) to finally catch on. I have a bitch puppy now and at the time of writing she has just begun to catch on and is now asking to go outside, but that is after four weeks of house training. Bracken, on the other hand, my basset hound crossbred, not only began asking to go out after a few days, but he was also clean at night after only a few days, which is quite impressive for an eight week old puppy. In view of this variance in response it is vital that we be patient when house training. This is true even after a puppy is clean in the home, as occasional accidents are not uncommon.

The procedure for house training is really quite simple. The puppy urinates or defecates, and this will no doubt be done on your best carpets, and all one has to do is immediately show the puppy the offending mess, tap it gently on the nose a few times with the end of your fingers, or even a folded thin magazine that will not hurt, while saying "no" in a firm voice that effectively transmits your displeasure, then carry the puppy outdoors while saying "outside" and put it down in the area where you want it to go.

Do not worry about your carpets. Use a good quality kitchen towel to soak up the urine or pick up the muck and then spray the area with a bottle of soapy water, or put disinfectant on a cloth and wipe and clean the area with this. Doing this will not only keep your carpet clean, but it will also stop the carpet from smelling. Back this up with the use of shake and vac or a similar product when hoovering and your carpet will remain fresh and clean.

It is important to be consistent and persistent when house training. You may feel tired after a hard day's work, or after seeing to the kids, but it is very important to carry out training after every offence. If you let puppies get away with it, even on occasion, then the lesson will take much longer to be learnt. It is also important to back this training up with helping your puppy to get into a routine of going outside. For instance after meals, and young puppies will usually have four meals a day, lead your puppy outside and give it a few minutes. Puppies will often defecate soon after meals, so it makes sense to allow them time outside after each meal. The same applies after the puppy has had a sleep. They will usually want to 'go' after a sleep, so it is a simple matter to lead them outside to do their business.

After every failure, transmit your displeasure and take the puppy outside, but after every success give plenty of praise, or even a little puppy treat, and this will not only save your carpet from much soiling, but it will help your puppy learn to go outside when it needs to 'go.' Again, be consistent and persistent and your efforts will be rewarded, but no time limit can be put on house training. Some learn very quickly, others take a few weeks to learn, or even months with some. I have never had a puppy that didn't learn to be clean in the home in the end. If one won't learn to be clean in the home, and this must be very rare if house training is carried out properly, then maybe such a dog would be best kept in a kennel, where there is obviously no need for house training.

The type of house training discussed is generally that around the home when the puppy is active. It is different at night. One can do nothing to prevent soiling in the night, but in the morning, when entering the room where the puppy is kept, or when loosing it from its cage, use the same method of showing it the mess, transmitting your displeasure in a way that is unpleasant, but not painful or abusive in any way, then lead it outside. They will learn to be clean at night in time, but this can take a while.

What will help a puppy to learn not to soil at night is firm and persistent daytime house training and showing your displeasure in the morning. Also, a good programme of regular exercise will also result in a clean floor or cage, as this will help the puppy sleep better and exercise will strengthen the bladder and bowel muscles so that they can hold it for a reasonable amount of time. Another good tip is to always allow your puppy time outside immediately before it goes to bed. This will help it to get into a routine of 'going' before settling down for the night.

If, after a reasonable period of time the youngster still isn't clean at night, try confining it to a space that allows it to sleep comfortably, but that doesn't allow it to wander about (I always keep mine in a dog cage at night, as this avoids mess in the home and prevents puppies from chewing furniture, floor covering, electric wires etc.). Many dogs and bitches will not soil their bed, especially when they get older, so this will teach them to hold it till morning. A young working terrier should thus be clean in the home during the day and at night by the age of six months or so (they will usually be clean during the day long before being clean at night), though some will take longer to be clean at night in particular, dog owners thus need to be patient until the lesson of house training is finally learnt.

16: THE INFLUENCE OF BORDER TERRIER BLOOD ON THE BREAY/BUCK STRAIN:

There are few working Border terriers these days, but in times past there were many working strains which had quite an influence on fell terrier breeding schemes generally, but especially on the working terriers bred by Cyril Breay and Frank Buck of High Casterton and Harmby respectively. Brian Nuttall can remember the fell terriers of the 1950s and 1960s and he states that most were partly bred from Border terriers. The earliest working Border terriers my researches have uncovered belonged to Alan Nelson of Gatesgarth Farm, Buttermere, which served with the Melbreak Foxhounds before and during Willie Irving's time at the hunt (pre-1926-1951, the Nelson family having bred Border terriers from at least the end of the 19th century, though they were more noted for breeding hard-coated old type Patterdale terriers from which the Border terrier and Lakeland terrier were founded on). Nelson's Border terriers, indirectly at least, had some influence on Cyril Breay and Frank Buck breeding policies, as did a working Border terrier strain kept by the Mitchell family of Cockermouth whose terriers also served with the Melbreak pack.

Willie Irving used Border terrier stud dogs on his Lakeland bitches in order to produce sensible, sane workers which could be used at otter and for badger digging without them being severely injured or killed because of having what terriermen call 'no reverse gears' – that is the inclination to close with otter or badger as they would a fox, with horrendous consequences. Irving's Lakeland terriers, all registered with the Kennel Club and all worked, would mostly kill foxes at the first opportunity and so Willie used Border terrier blood because this breed was known for its sensible qualities. Cyril Breay and Frank Buck used such blood for similar reasons. The country both Breay and Buck hunted required a harder fox killing type of terrier, but what Border terrier influence produced was a terrier that would bolt foxes, especially reluctant foxes run in by hounds, while also being capable of killing a fox that remained below ground. Both Breay and Buck produced many great bolting terriers with much sense, such as Tex, Chew, Twig, Tig, Nip, Kitty, Gem and Skiffle, to mention just a few. True, some were just too hard, lacking sense and being hysterically keen to latch onto fox, badger and otter and receiving serious injuries as a result, but, generally speaking Breay and Buck terriers were incredibly useful, especially in the north where deep rock earths abound.

Major Burdon of the Bedale Foxhounds in North Yorkshire bred a superb working strain of Border terrier (Brian Nuttall believes this strain had just a dash of fell terrier in its pedigree, though that is true of most, if not all Border terriers of the 1940s and 1950s) which often ran loose with hounds. Frank Buck used at least one of these Burdon Border terrier stud dogs on his bitch Tiger and this line greatly influenced Breay/Buck bloodlines from the early 1940s onwards. Jossie Akerigg of Garsdale – a superb breeder of working terriers and an expert at hunting and catching foxes – also used Border terrier blood out of the Burdon strain. Akerigg's terriers partly influenced Cyril Breay and Frank Buck terrier breeding schemes, as did the Border terriers of Joe Dobbinson of the Zetland Foxhounds, who also bred a superb working strain of Border terrier that proved to be great fox bolting terriers, though some would kill a fox that wouldn't bolt. Dobbinson's terriers were also quick to enter, which was unusual, as many Border terrier strains, even during the 1940s and 1950s, were rather slow to start, but were great workers once they entered. Many of Joe Dobbinson's Border terriers had to be held back and one he bred killed a fox at just seven months of age.

Major Williams of Sedbergh was a keen breeder of working Border terriers which saw service at all large quarry, often working with the Kendal and District Otterhounds and other packs. At a time when badger digging was legal and considered as a respectable means of pest control, Major Williams organised badger digs in the Cumbrian and Yorkshire Dales and Cyril

Breay often attended these, so it is possible, even likely, that Breay occasionally resorted to outcross blood by using one of Major Williams' Border terrier stud dogs, though I have no proof of this. Cyril Breay would use any stud dog that impressed him and the Border terriers bred by Major Williams produced some great workers, so Breay would surely have no objections to such bloodlines entering his strain. Especially did Breay use Border terrier blood to correct problems he had with bad mouths in his terriers. Border terriers have not only produced excellent coat, but such blood produced good strong heads and powerful jaws too – qualities Breay desired in his terriers. John Park confirmed that Border terrier blood entered the strain after Breay purchased a very hard Border terrier from Robson of Carlisle, which Breay used on his bitches, producing some wonderful workers.

I mentioned earlier that the Breay/Buck strains were indirectly influenced by Alan Nelson's and Mitchell's strains of Border terrier (which were very likely related). That is because Willie Irving used Nelson's and Mitchell's Border terriers early on in the breeding of his Lakeland terriers, which he registered with the Kennel Club when the Lakeland became a recognised breed during the 1920s. Breay and Buck used Irving bloodlines on their strains through Joe Wear's Tear 'Em and Harry Hardisty's Turk (Both Breay and Buck used Tear 'Em and Turk several times on their bitches), both these terriers being bred out of Irving Lakeland terriers (the vast majority of fell and Patterdale terriers today are descended from Willie Irving's strain of Lakeland terrier). Also, the sire of Bingo was a terrier belonging to Robinson of Cockermouth, which was undoubtedly at least partly-bred out of Irving strain Lakeland terriers (very few terriers in the Lakes during the 1960s were not bred this way). Breay and Buck frequently bred back to Tear 'Em and Turk bloodlines in order to improve type in their stock and so the Nelson strain of Border terrier had its influence on their breeding policies via this route. It is thus clear to see that Border terrier bloodlines have greatly influenced the rootstock of today's Patterdale terriers through the hard work and careful breeding schemes of both Cyril Breay and Frank Buck, not to mention other important breeders such as Brian Nuttall and Jossic Akcrigg.

17: HOUND INTELLIGENCE & WORKING TERRIERS:
Our hard working packs are full of interesting characters which lighten the days of those who work with them and the kennel where I worked had more

than enough characters to make my work more enjoyable, even the mundane everyday tasks, but what stands out most, particularly in the hunting field, is just how intelligent hounds can be.

This intelligence at work is obvious and is no better demonstrated at dense coverts, or, in the case of the fell packs and those packs which hunt other mountainous regions such as in Wales. Before the Hunting Act in England and Wales, these mountain packs hunted fox in incredibly arduous conditions and foxes often took them on long hunts, while using every trick in the book to try to throw hounds off. One such trick was to climb steep and dangerous crags where more often than not hounds couldn't follow. In this instance hounds would, of their own volition, climb out around the crags, one lot going around one side, while the other lot would go around the other, hounds meeting at the top so that, had the fox stolen away, every part of the fell around the crags would have been covered. Sometimes the fox would have gone out at the top of the crag and what a spectacular sight to see hounds meet at the top and hit off the line again, their cry sounding and resounding from the high fells. There was nothing more thrilling than to hear a pack of mountain hounds going in full cry on a good scenting day.

It surely shows that hounds have a marked degree of intelligence when they are capable of working out for themselves that casting around the crag will help them pick up the line again or reveal that the fox is sheltering on a crag ledge (a 'bink' or 'benk' in Lakeland parlance).

Hounds that hunt the shires have also demonstrated great intelligence in similar ways. Many hunts planted very low growing gorse or furze coverts during earlier centuries and, while these proved great as fox holding coverts, they also proved nigh-on impossible for hounds to get into in order to push out a fox skulking there. On arriving at such dense coverts whilst hunting a fox, hounds would act in a similar manner to the fell packs at a crag. True, a few hounds would try to push on through such dense gorse coverts and sometimes succeeded, but the majority of the pack would cast around both sides of the gorse in order to discern if the fox had gone through and had gone away, or in order to discover that Charlie had remained in covert. If the fox would not leave and hounds couldn't get in, then a good finding terrier would have been used to flush the fox and Parson Russell, when hunting his hounds in the North Devon area, often used his famous terriers at coverts where hounds struggled to get in.

Hounds sometimes use their intelligence in order to get extra helpings of food. Fell Foxhounds are notorious for their intelligence and in the old days when the packs were walked to their various hunting grounds, staying in different areas and hunting those districts for a week at a time, the huntsmen often had problems with hounds stealing food along the way. For instance, it is well documented that Joe Bowman usually cycled from kennels to the farm or inn where the Ullswater Foxhounds were to stay for a week of hunting, obviously using the roads on the valley floors and passes over the fells whilst doing so, which meant that he often cycled past villages and farms along the way. Bowman was a famous huntsman who knew how to turn out a fit and hard-hunting pack of hounds, but he knew that his control of an intelligent pack of hounds constantly on the look-out for titbits of food was limited to some degree, so he would cycle through villages and past farms rather rapidly, calling on his hounds whilst doing so, yet a few of the hounds would sneak into farm and cottage kitchens and steal food at every opportunity and many a good cake, joint of meat, or loaf of bread went missing when hounds came through, or passed-by a farm. Bowman would flee, cycling like a madman away from farms and villages blowing his horn, whilst many a housewife ranted and raved at hounds running away with their food. In spite of this, the fell pack huntsmen were greatly respected in the Lakes and every farm and village would be happy to have hounds and huntsmen stay.

One of our own hounds is not only intelligent when it comes to obtaining a little bit of extra food, but he has proven to be very athletic. Our grass-yard where hounds can relax, play, or dig, doing wonders for their mental well-being, is at the back of the kennels and three of our kennels border it. We use one of them for flesh when we have a surplus and Garrison had worked-out a way of getting over the bars and into the kennel. He was also proving difficult to leave behind on a hunting day, as he worked out how to get over the bars of the main kennel and would run after the hunt lorry. Fortunately, Garrison was a keen and eager hunter and went very well on trail-scent, so he was rarely left behind anyway.

One of the most impressive displays of intelligence was by a Bleasdale beagle several years ago when he failed to return at the end of a hunting day and had to be left behind. Although hunt staff searched for him, the hound wasn't found and after a few days hope of finding him was fading, but two weeks later he turned up at the kennels having covered many miles and having crossed several busy roads safely. Such occurrences, which can be repeated several times over, aptly demonstrate just how intelligent our working hounds can be.

18: WORKING TERRIER RESCUES:

Scamp was a five year old terrier belonging to Frank Buck of Harmby near Leyburn in North Yorkshire and this terrier, on loan to local fox catcher Jack Kilburn, was put to ground after a livestock killing fox in a rock hole on the fells between Askrigg in Wensleydale, made famous as the setting for Darrowby in the original series of *All Creatures Great and Small*, and Carperby, where Alf Wight (author James Herriot) and his wife Joan (Helen) spent their honeymoon in 1942. Scamp was renowned for his sense when working fox to ground and by this time had earned a reputation for being superb at his work, a reputation that was common to many of Buck's Breay-bred terriers.

Scamp found his fox and he was still working to ground when darkness came on and so Jack Kilburn was forced to leave the terrier to ground and was back at first light the next morning in order to see how Scamp was getting on. Unfortunately, the terrier, for whatever reason, had become trapped and so digging commenced that day and Frank Buck tried blasting the unyielding rock, but only succeeded in dislodging a huge chunk of rock, which then fell across the hole they had been digging, hampering greatly any further efforts to dig Scamp out of that fortress earth. In those days (this rescue occurred in March 1950 and at the same time Mister John Pyman, Master of the Goathland Hunt, was in the process of rescuing his terrier Wendy, another great worker, from a rock hole on the North York Moors, having had to resort to dynamite after several days of attempting to effect a rescue) caving clubs were occasionally called upon to help rescue a terrier and on this occasion the Settle Caving Club was called in, as even Frank Buck was stumped after his failed blasting attempt, a technique he learned from local quarrymen.

Using their expertise at negotiating very tight caves underground, the cavers eventually succeeded in reaching Scamp and they fetched him out on the fourth day of the rescue, much to everyone's relief. Scamp had lost two pounds in weight, two teeth and had been bitten during the encounter, but the report fails to state whether or not the fox was recovered, though I think it very likely.

May 1949 witnessed the Blencathra Foxhounds, with George Bell hunting hounds in his very last season, with Johnny Richardson about to take over after whipping-in since 1946, out hunting for a lamb-killing fox in the Borrowdale Valley and the culprit was soon found and run to ground, in a rock hole on the fells. Rock and Sambo were entered and they soon killed the fox, very quickly and very effectively putting an end to the farmer's losses to his livelihood. However, in the process of tackling and killing the fox, the two terriers became trapped and thus digging commenced. In the Lake District, it was traditional to dig out the carcass of a fox worried in by terriers, which tradition harked back to the days when bounty money could be claimed on every fox brush presented to the local Church Warden. When terriers were trapped, the Lakeland hunters went to great lengths in order to recover them and they mostly succeeded. No less effort was put into this rescue, but after three days of shifting rock and earth, although the noses of the terriers could just be seen sixteen feet into the fellside, unyielding rocks meant that the tunnel was too narrow for a grown man to negotiate. In such situations brave young lads were sometimes called upon and now nine year old Jimmy Pepper was keen to take part in what would be his second terrier rescue that season.

Jimmy was from an illustrious family of terriermen. His grandfather was Jack Pepper, who bred the Bowderstone strain of Lakeland terrier that saw service with the Blencathra and Melbreak Foxhounds and which had earned a reputation second to none as workers, as well as lookers, for many a show was won by this strain of improved Lakeland terrier. Jimmy's father was Frank 'Pont' Pepper, who continued to breed the Bowderstone strain and who was a friend of Willie Irving. Willie used the Bowderstone studs on his own Lakeland bitches and often worked some of the Bowderstone Lakelands for the Pepper family. Bowderstone Turk, for instance, was on loan to Willie Irving, which terrier belonged to Frank Pepper. Frank also worked his terriers with the 'Cathra and so was always on hand if a rescue was necessary. Frank Pepper, like his father Jack, was a quarryman and he worked at the infamous Honister Quarries at this time, living at Seatoller, close to the foot of the spectacular Honister Pass, which meant that his expertise at working rock was invaluable during a rescue. It seems that Jimmy was a natural when it came to working rock too, as he crawled into the narrow tunnel and eventually succeeded in fetching out Sambo on the third day of operations. Rock wouldn't leave the dead fox and so had to be left in for another night, but Jimmy got him out the next morning and the newspapers reported the event, making young Jimmy a bit of a 'celebrity' at the time.

The following rescue was quite unusual in the sense that, although three terriers were involved, none had actually gone to ground. During April 1929 the Melbreak Foxhounds were hunting below 300-foot high crags, while their huntsman, Willie Irving, stood on top watching his pack working below. Three terriers got over-excited and they fell over the crags, with one being killed, while the other two survived the fall. Risking his life, Willie then climbed down the crags, without a rope attached to him it has to be noted, and successfully rescued the two surviving terriers. Many opposers of hunting claim that those who work terriers, hounds, lurchers etc do not care about their dogs. What rubbish! These and hundreds of other rescues certainly demonstrate just how much such men and women do care, as massive and thorough efforts to rescue terriers etc are aways carried out and such rescuers never give up until every method of effecting a rescue has been exhausted.

19: MEMORIES OF FOXHUNTING WITH A TERRIER PACK:

Before the infamous hunting ban that came into effect in 2005, I had built a small pack of terriers that was often supplemented with small hounds such as teckels, as well as a number of beagle crossbreds, with which I carried out necessary pest control for farmers and sometimes gamekeepers, while at the same time enjoying some great days of superb hound and terrier work. I could easily fill a good-sized book with my hunting in those days. One of those hunting days stands out as one of the best, which was a good mix of terrier work and hunting above ground.

  Just like any pack of foxhounds, I spent late August through to the end of October drawing mostly dense coverts in order to disperse litters of fox cubs that would stick together and often hunt in packs otherwise. And when cubs (which by late August are more or less fully grown and able to fend for themselves, their mother having left them by this time) stay and hunt together they can kill huge numbers of chickens kept at farms and smallholdings and very occasionally they will take to killing lambs that, by late summer, have put on quite a bit of growth. This is by no means common, but it does happen and I have seen lambs killed at this time of year by hungry cubs 'packing,' so dispersing young foxes during late summer and autumn is essential, but in England and Wales must now be done with just two hounds, which makes the task impossible to be frank. And so, during the late summer of 2003 or 4, I can't just pinpoint the exact year, I was out on my own with my pack of fell terriers, intent on dispersing a litter of cubs from a wood at the gateway to a long, wide valley where I have had permission for many years, thanks to my one-time hunting partner, the late Roy Pilling; a very keen and knowledgeable countryman who was also a very talented mechanic.

Roy fixed tractors and other farm machinery and obtained thousands of acres of permission for us while doing so. Together with the permission I obtained, we built a huge hunting country and hunted a variety of quarry, predominantly foxes, as farmers wanted their numbers controlled in order to prevent or reduce losses to their livestock. We readily helped them out, of course.

A fine early September morning saw me drawing the rush-beds above the wood in question and I noticed Turk slip away from the pack and drop into the wood where he knew there was a stone drain that sometimes holds foxes. It held this day alright, as he went to ground and quickly bolted a litter of four cubs. Two headed south into the depths of the wood and two came out of the wood and headed into a very dense area of rushes, trying to stay together.

Turk hunted the line and I cast the rest of the pack into the rush-bed. The pack got together and found the two foxes skulking among the rushes, flushing one south and the other north. Turk went on the northerly fox, while the rest of the pack, led by Fell, went on the southerly fox, which left me with a bit of a dilemma. I quickly decided to follow the northerly fox, as there were dense woods to the south and I wanted to head for the valley head and surrounding moors, while encouraging the rest of the pack to abandon their southerly fox and hunt this one instead, which is exactly what they did when they checked. It was dry and getting warm in the late summer sun by now, so I knew scenting conditions would be difficult, which proved to be the case. I eventually got all of them onto the northerly fox and they hunted well in the rising sunshine, but it was never a 'screaming' scent. It was a steady hunt with a few checks along the way, till they finally caught up with Turk in some vast bracken-beds at the head of the valley, the steep sides of the hills leading up to the long lines of crags and old stone workings, then upwards to the wind-ravaged moors beyond.

Foxes will very often try to stay in large coverts and the smaller the pack the more difficult it is to persuade them to leave such safe hiding places, but after chasing and hunting their fox about these bracken-beds for quite some time, the scent having improved where the sun couldn't reach the ground, Charlie finally decided to vacate the premises and made up the steep hillside and then swung left, making through the old stone workings, across the ghyll and away to the crags on the opposite side, where Charlie went to ground in a notoriously bad place. Only Turk got away on the line and I was glad to see him struggling more and more on the rapidly fading scent, the strong sun now evaporating scent very quickly. I have seen terriers work this crag earth successfully in the past, but I had stopped working it due to others having lost terriers there over the years, so I was relieved to be able to blow Turk back to me before he reached the crag.

Although no foxes had been accounted for, I had achieved my aim; that of dispersing this litter. It was unlikely they would pack again, but if they did it didn't matter, as I would be hunting here again in the near future, hoping to reduce the number of foxes in the area for the sake of wildlife such as ground-nesting birds and, of course, the local farmers.

20: JOE BOWMAN & HIS ULLSWATER HOUNDS:

Joe Bowman is a legendary figure in fell-hunting history and rightly so, as he spent most of his days with hounds and became a legend in his own lifetime, which few achieve, even in this modern world where it seems some folk need to accomplish very little, and have even less talent, in order to become a so-called celebrity. Joe Bowman, like John Peel before him, did become a sort of celebrity in the Lakes and particularly in the country his Ullswater hounds hunted, and he was thus highly respected and even revered by many. His Mardale Meets became famous countrywide and many attended, mostly for the hunting of course, which was fabulous and action-packed much of the time, but also for the 'harvels' or celebrations held during this special event.

Joe Bowman was born into a mining and hunting family and, although he spent much of his youth hunting with his uncles, the Dawsons, Joe spent some time as a farmhand for the Dalemain Estate, the main house being situated along the Pooley Bridge/Penrith road only a spitting distance from Ullswater. This estate is also steeped in hunting history and staghounds once hunted red deer on Dalemain land, which was once incredibly vast in area and included the remote valley of Martindale, where possibly polecats and pinemartens just about hung onto existence after becoming extinct in the rest of England.

Joe then had a stint as a miner at the famous lead mines in the valley close to Glenridding, but his opportunity to get out of the mines soon came along when the newly formed Ullswater Foxhounds became in need of a huntsman. Joe had been very useful in both the farming and mining trades, as he proved to be very strong and fit and his stamina soon made him stand out among his contemporaries and get attention from those who worked with him. That strength, fitness and stamina, undoubtedly developed when out hunting as a youth with both the Matterdale and Patterdale Foxhounds, which merged in the summer of 1878 to become the Ullswater Foxhounds, stood him in good stead when applying for the job as huntsman, as all of those qualities are essential when hunting a mountain pack of hounds, which covered several miles in an average day's hunting – the huntsman having to keep up with his pack as best he could.

Joe had a very successful start to his hunting career and his first hunt of real note was fittingly at the Mardale Meet in the November of 1878. The hunt began in the morning and took in several fells until the fox went to ground close to Buck Crag, the final stages of the hunt taking place in the moonlight of that autumn evening. Bowman found hounds marking eagerly, but deemed it best to leave the fox for another day, though this mammoth hunt earned him much respect from the many followers who flocked to Mardale each year. Someone once said that foxes are killed in kennels and this is very true when it comes to fell-hounds in particular, as this saying simply means that good kennel management; turning out a pack in excellent health and fitness, was vital if hounds were to succeed in controlling foxes among such difficult and arduous terrain. Joe Bowman quickly earned a reputation for his expert kennel management skills and his pack were always turned out in top condition – well fed and fit for purpose – anything less would have seen him lose his job in no time at all.

Another great hunt was towards the end of his first season, during the closing days of winter 1879. A fox in fine condition was roused near Gowbarrow Hall, which took hounds through Watermillock and on towards Matterdale, through the Glencoyne area. Scent was good and the pace 'rattling' as he set his mask for Matterdale Common, but hounds turned him towards Latterbarrow. Towler, Lecturer, Clasher and Roguery were just a few of the hounds proving to be most useful during this hunt so far and after a long hunt they forced him to make for Glenridding Screes. Hounds turned him again and he went close to Black Crag and back towards Glencoyne. He now passed some cottages and made for the main road skirting Ullswater, but then climbed a hill off the Patterdale Road, before being turned again and headed back to the main road, which he crossed. Hounds really pressed him here as they hunted through some rocky ground. 'Jacky' then took to the lake and hounds plunged in after him, killing him in the water after a hard and very fast hunt of two hours. This hunt unquestionably demonstrates that Joe Bowman knew how to turn out a fit and healthy pack of hounds that could 'live' with any fox on those bleak and rugged fells. His future as a first-class huntsman, it seems, was already secure by the end of that first season.

Clasher and Roguery were superb hunting hounds which often led the pack and at the end of that season, in the early spring of 1879, these two hounds played a vital role in a mammoth hunt which started in Grasmere, took in the Borrowdale Valley, over into Buttermere and then over the fells into Ennerdale. The end result wasn't known as nobody could keep up that day, but hounds made their own way back to their huntsman, with three missing, Clasher, Roguery and Lucifer. Lucifer lodged with someone and was returned to kennels, Roguery eventually turned up, but poor Clasher had been killed on a railway line while making his way home. Bowman soon learned that hunting a pack of fell hounds wasn't always joyful, as some days did end in tragedy, though these were thankfully few and far between.

Bowman bred some incredibly game terriers, as well as wonderfully gifted hunting hounds, Cleaver being possibly his best-ever hound, though many of his earth dogs were on loan from various followers; miners, farmers and gentry included. Jack, Lil, Turk, Wasp, Grip, Fury, Tan, Dick, Spider, Nancie, Rose, Nip, Corby and Tatters are just a few of Bowman's terriers to make a name for themselves, but there were many more and few terriers in the Lakes at that time and on into the future did not have the blood of Bowman's stock running through their veins.

Joe Bowman retired in 1924 and he enjoyed close association with his beloved pack until his death in 1940. Hundreds attended his funeral and this event went down in fell history as one of the great occasions, such was the respect people had for him, as his fame had spread nationwide due to his exploits and the publicity they attracted. Joe Bowman was quite simply a legend and he remains so to this day.

21: DEALING WITH THE SLOW STARTER:

Speaking from experience, there is possibly nothing more frustrating for a terrierman than a working terrier that just will not enter to quarry, or enters, but in a sort of half-hearted way. I have seen novice terriers completely refuse to enter to quarry, while others have gone to a fox, but have quickly come off their quarry after a few bays. If such behaviour persists, then a terrier can be labelled a slow starter and great patience and perseverance is needed in such a situation. Nowadays one must try to work terriers within the law of the country in which you reside, but still, large quarry is worked by many terriermen and so foxes present a challenge to any young terrier just starting.

A slow starter must not be confused with a terrier that is simply inexperienced and doesn't quite settle to earth work in particular at first. True, some terriers, if allowed to fully mature mentally and physically before going to a fox, will enter immediately and work foxes properly from day one. Many strains of fell and Lakeland terrier, for instance, enter very quickly. Joe Wear's Tear 'Em, for example, from out of a bitch bred by Willie Irving and actually owned by Jim Fleming of Grasmere, being on loan at the Ullswater Foxhounds during the latter half of the 1940s and early part of the 1950s, entered to his first fox and killed it after receiving an initial bite from the fox. However, many terriers just do not start in such a spectacular manner.

Ghyll was one such terrier, in spite of being bred down from Cyril Breay's Bingo line. Long before the Hunting Act I had a fox to ground in quite a deep stone drain and was digging it with Rock. Ghyll was about fifteen months of age at the time, which is generally the age at which I enter novice terriers to fox. He was pinned down outside and could hear Rock hard at the fox, so I slipped him in to see what he would do. I expected him to enter and go like wildfire, but he simply joined in for a few bays and then emerged. I admit that I was disappointed, but carried on the dig regardless and left Ghyll for another day. He next had a few stints to ground alone and bolted a number of foxes, till one day he entered a moorland earth and really got stuck into a fox which wouldn't bolt. He killed a large dog fox single-handed and never looked back. With hindsight, it would have been better had I waited until he had matured a little more before trying him on a dig, as he very naturally settled to his work once he was ready to do so. Patience is needed in such a situation, but Ghyll was not what one would consider a slow starter, as he quickly progressed in his work.

Mocky, on the other hand, was a slow starter and she was given ample opportunity to enter to fox by her owner, the late Tim Poxton, who was a good terrierman by any standards. Tim had some very useful terriers over the years and was at one time terrierman to the Holcombe Hunt, though he also carried out fox control for farmers in the Rossendale Valley area, as well as some fox control work for gamekeepers in Staffordshire. Tim tried Mocky on many occasions during fox digs to his other excellent working terriers, but she showed no interest whatsoever. She would go to ground and run through earths, but would completely ignore any fox skulking below ground. At one large earth in the hills above Bacup, Tim put Mocky to ground after his other terriers had shown interest and she ran the earth, emerging after a few minutes. Tim then tried one of his other terriers, which soon found a fox and settled, the terrier and fox later being dug out. Mocky had severely tried Tim's patience by this time and he weighed up the situation, deciding that she would have to go. However, he persevered a little longer with Mocky and gave her one last opportunity to enter.

He was out with the Holcombe Hunt after a meet at the Bull's Head at Greenmount near Ramsbottom and a fox was roused in the low country, which took to Holcombe Moor where Peel Tower dominates the skyline and hounds hunted their fox across the face of the hill, going through deep heather and over the screes left there from much quarrying activity of former centuries. Hounds went with a great cry and followed their fox to an old quarry above the northern end of Holcombe Village. There they eagerly marked a hole at the top of the crags of the quarry. Tim couldn't remember exactly why he decided to try Mocky in such a situation, but with the hunt staff and followers watching, Tim put in his bitch Mocky and, as usual, she went to ground eagerly. This is quite a well-known earth which has held many foxes over the years. It is also very deep and only a quality terrier could succeed in shifting a fox, especially one that has been hunted by hounds and is reluctant to move, so Tim, as one can imagine, began to wonder if he had done the right thing.

After several minutes of the bitch working through the earth, she at last began to bay and quickly bolted the fox, which got away by crossing the main road and making its way down to the edge of Ramsbottom where hounds couldn't hope to follow. Mocky never looked back after that and she became a very useful worker, which also bred some excellent working terriers, with Zak being just about one of the best terriers she produced. Zak was a wonderful finder and killer of foxes, even in the deep and dangerous old mine-workings found in the hills surrounding the industrial towns of Lancashire and Yorkshire. I was fortunate enough to hunt with Zak on numerous occasions. Unlike his mother, Zak entered quickly to fox. His sister, however, like her mother, took an age to enter, but became a useful worker once she caught on. Patience and perseverance are necessary qualities when it comes to working terriers which prove to be slow starters, but given time and opportunity, many of these eventually become superb workers, so exercising such patience and perseverance may be well worth it in the end.

22: A FEW HAIR-RAISING DIGS:
There have been many digs to terrier and fox that can be described as 'hair-raising' and probably digs in borrans and rockpiles in old quarries have been some of the most difficult and dangerous of all, but sand earths have

produced several digs where close calls have been common. Sadly, many a valiant terrier has suffocated in sand and the manner in which a terrier will work, in itself puts them in a certain amount of danger in this type of fox den. When a working terrier comes to a tight spot, or a fox gets itself into a particularly tight stop-end, not only will a terrier dig, in its eagerness to get up to the fox, but it will bite at anything in its way, including tree-roots, ripping large amounts of earth away in the process and getting soil and sand stuck in its mouth. If a terrier continues to do this and it cannot clear the sand from its mouth, then it becomes so full as to prevent the dog from breathing in what is already restricted airspace to some extent. And so the poor terrier can suffocate, though such an occurrence is not that common.

There are a few sand holes in the country I hunt, but they are quite rare and are easily avoided, though not all sand earths are that dangerous to work. If the earth is shallow and a terrier can be got out quickly (in places and circumstances where terrier work remains legal), then working sand is relatively safe enough, but deep places are best avoided. True, the terrierman cannot always judge the depth of an earth, though often much can be learned about a variety of earths from experienced terriermen in the area. Many earths have been worked by generations of terriermen and those places best avoided are usually passed on by word of mouth.

If a sand earth is on the deep side, then not only is the terrier in danger of not being dug out in time should it get into trouble, but the diggers can be in a certain amount of danger from the sand above collapsing onto them, especially if they have to dig a shaft into a hillside or steep bank (props should always be used on such deep digs, to keep the roof of the dig from falling in). Willie Irving of the Melbreak Foxhounds was once digging into a railway embankment in low country on the western fringes of Lorton Vale, after his terrier, Mick of Millar Place, one of his best workers during the late 1940s and early 1950s, had engaged and bottled-up a fox. Willie tunnelled into the embankment and whilst working inside the roof of the dig, which happened to be a sand earth, it collapsed on him. Thankfully some of the hunt followers were in attendance and assisting the huntsman, so they were able to pull him out by his feet. Willie then went on to successfully and safely dig to Mick and the fox, which had earlier been run-in by hounds.

The trouble with sand is that one cannot always tell it is a sand earth, as the first few inches may well be soil. I have dug a few earths that have started off as soil, but then as I have dug down it has changed to sand. One such earth is where Turk killed a fox without incident, as this earth, situated in a valley on the edge of the West Pennines above Ramsbottom, was only shallow. Fell killed a fox in the same earth, but I was forced to leave him in overnight, as darkness came on and he had become trapped behind the carcass. I was back first thing the next morning and had him and the very dead fox out of there within half-an-hour.

Another earth I have worked over the years is close to the River Roch near Heywood in Lancashire. This was yet another safe sand earth to work, as it was shallow, but large in area. There were about five or six holes to this place, spread out over quite a wide area and foxes used to fly out of there. My bitch Mist, a rather typey Patterdale terrier with a slape coat (slape means slippery in Lakeland parlance and is used when describing a very dense, smooth coat as found on many Patterdale and fell terriers), entered the earth when running loose after bushing rabbits from briars, which grow all over this area, and she bolted a large dog fox which came flying out of the earth in spectacular style, like shot from a canon.

The famous terrierman John Park has had some success working sand holes and he was telling me about one memorable dig to a dog of his called Blackie. This wasn't a particularly deep spot, but it proved to be quite a dig and as he went along John uncovered one dead fox after another until, finally, breaking through to Blackie who was at the stop-end with two more foxes, one of which he had killed and the other he was just finishing off. Digging in sand is always hair-raising, as there is always the worry of suffocation, but Blackie didn't need to dig on to his foxes, so, barring roof collapses, he was quite safe.

The late Joe Armstrong, as good a terrierman as one could wish to meet, once lost one of his Willie Irving bred terriers in sand, while digging badger on a railway embankment near Carlisle in the 1950s. The terrier had dug on and had thus bitten huge chunks of sand out of the tight tunnel walls in the process, its mouth so full of sand that it couldn't breathe and thus suffocation was inevitable.

One of the best digs in sand I have enjoyed was to Rock and Pep when Roy Pilling and I were hunting a small wood in the hills above Bury and Ramsbottom, not far from a small village, or maybe hamlet would better describe it, called Nangreaves. The terriers went to earth and it proved to be sand, but Roy and I managed to safely dig out the terriers and fox without incident, in spite of the fact that the sand was collapsing in places as we dug on, which was rather hair-raising and we were glad to get the terriers out safely in the end.

23: HISTORIC HUNTING WITH THE BLENCATHRA FOXHOUNDS:

Before the death of Squire Crozier in 1903, who was the Blencathra Foxhounds long serving and popular master, huntsman Jim Dalton answered a lamb worrying call and loosed his pack near Walla Crag above Derwentwater as dawn was breaking, only a stone's-throw away from the small and busy town of Keswick, which in those days was bustling with miners, farmers and tourists. Local farmers had been losing lambs to a fell fox and so Dalton tried under the crag and hounds struck a drag and took it through the woodlands and past Ashness Bridge, where the views of Derwentwater and Skiddaw are incredible, this bridge reputedly being the most photographed spot in the Lake District.

The drag took them all the way to lovely and lonely Watendlath and it was here that Reynard was found lying out above ground. Hounds followed the early morning scent as it led them past High Seat and over the fell tops to Armboth, hunting their quarry above Thirlmere Lake and heading to Raven Crag and thence on to the rough screes above the lake. Reynard then led past Smeathwaite and to the strangely named Worm Crag, then he flew down Williams Ghyll as he was pressed by hounds.

The music was breathtaking as hounds ran in full cry, their sound echoing and fading among the high crags and deep valleys of the fell country, echoing and fading repeatedly as hounds stuck to their fox. The fox then made through the Naddle Valley and climbed for Causeway Pike, by Scott Howe. He then made through woodland and away across Bleaberry Fell, making, it was thought, for Gate Crag and sanctuary, but again hounds pressed their fox hard and he changed his course and crossed Southwaite Ghyll instead, climbing the Benn and slinking into a strong borran or bield (bield means shelter in fell parlance) in this area, which was not an easy spot for terriers, yet Banter and Pincher were entered and they followed their fox eagerly. These were game terriers and Banter in particular carved out quite a reputation as a working terrier.

This pair of game terriers soon found their fox and put so much pressure on it that it decided to make a run for it and bolted soon after, with hounds once again getting onto the line and hunting a strong scent with great cry. Reynard made for the top of the Benn, with Stormer, Charmer and Comely close on his brush and putting so much pressure on him that he now made down the fells for Naddle Bottoms, with hounds in full cry and the fox unable to shake them off, no matter what cunning tricks he tried. The fox was now showing signs of having been hunted over a huge distance, yet he still crossed and made onto High Rigg, but the pace of the hounds was just too great and shortly afterwards Miller pulled him down and ended the race, with the rest of the pack quickly on the scene, their cry having never failed throughout. It had been a spectacular hunt and one that helped secure the fame of Jim Dalton, the huntsman who served at the Blencathra Hunt from 1894 until 1930, when he passed the horn to George Bell.

Jim Dalton was from a farming family at Caldbeck and he very quickly established himself as one of the finest huntsmen the Lake District has ever produced. His pace across the fells as he followed his pack was said to be nigh-on impossible to keep with. He had incredible stamina too and one long hunt ended with the fox going to ground in among rocks on the side of a Borrowdale ghyll late in the day, when a terrier was put in, as, typically, it wasn't long before Dalton caught up with his pack, in spite of the distances travelled. The terrier engaged the fox and worked with gusto, but Reynard wouldn't, or possibly couldn't bolt and so digging commenced, but this was a bad place for digging out and so operations continued by lamplight during the hours of darkness and it was several hours before at last fox and terrier were reached and extricated from that bad earth. The villagers of Borrowdale could see the flickering lamplight on the fellside as the diggers grafted late into the night in order to get to the terrier working its fox below.

Another long hunt was at Mungrisedale; a historic place long associated with great days with the Blencathra Foxhounds, and again Dalton was in charge, though many years later, during the early winter of 1923. Hounds had their fox afoot and it took them away to Tarn Crag and down Bowscale Fell, giving them a good and fast hunt to Brock Crag, where Charlie went to earth in rocks, but a chap named Cockbain soon landed at the spot and put in his terrier bitch, which had made a name for herself as a game fox dog. That terrier bitch soon found and persuaded the fox to bolt and it came out of the rocks like a shot from a gun, with hounds in pursuit, hunting it through woodlands and out onto open fell, where at last they accounted for their quarry. Cockbain must have been very pleased with his brave and stout-hearted terrier, as she was a great worker of foxes and that particular fox, under pressure, exited swiftly, despite having been hunted hard by hounds above ground. The Blencathra Foxhounds did very well to account for a lamb worrying fox during what was a long and fast hunt, at a time of year when scent could be difficult due to extremely cold conditions on the fells. Jim Dalton must have been pleased with his gallant pack, which was famed for hunting and catching foxes, though during Squire Crozier's time in particular, hounds also hunted hares, polecats, pinemartens and even carted deer (these deer were released and later caught again unharmed, once they had laid the scent for hounds to hunt).

☀

24: SCENT, HOUNDS & DRIFT MINES:

"There's nowt so queer as scent" is a famous and oft-quoted saying that is founded on more than an element of truth, as scent is probably one of the most unpredictable forces on the planet. The late Johnny Richardson, long-serving and popular huntsman of the Blencathra Foxhounds, would state that if the stones, or rocks, were wet, then scent would be good. In view of Johnny Richardson's great success and experience as a huntsman, one is compelled to respect what he said, but in my own experience there are no set rules where scent is concerned and while many days with the stones wet will produce good scenting, I have also known other days when scent is poor, in spite of the fact that the stones were wet.

 Wet and mild generally produces good scenting, but in my experience it all depends on the amount of rainfall we get, not to mention how mild it is. If torrential rain sets in and the ground becomes waterlogged, then scent will usually be poor. Also, higher temperatures much above ten or twelve degrees will mean that scent dies quite quickly. Bright sunshine and blustery weather will kill scent quickly too, but it is not that easy to predict scent quality, no matter what the conditions. Such days can be very frustrating. I have seen, on a number of occasions actually, hares or foxes getting up and going away while hounds were drawing nearby and, when the huntsman has laid on his pack, they have gone away on a screaming scent for maybe fifty or seventy-five yards and then scent has simply disappeared, seemingly into thin air, never to be recovered, in spite of some good circular casting.

 I have also seen hounds pick up a line and go really well, but then after a good few minutes they have lifted their heads and have gone wide of the original line as the scent begins to evaporate into the air and drift on the breeze. In such situations one can then be certain that hounds will lose the line within a few minutes. This happened one day when hunting on the fells of North Yorkshire. Two hares got up fifty yards ahead of hounds and went away in opposite directions, the hounds speaking eagerly while the hare was in view, the cry still great to hear, when at last the hare disappeared over the crest of the hill and hounds finally got their noses down, going well on what was obviously a good scent. Hounds hunted very well across the fell, having just one check and putting themselves right after putting in a good circular cast, going away again to a gate and through, their pilot now taking them onto an old fell road used by shepherds, quarrymen and miners when these fells were extensively worked. Hounds stuck to the scent along this old road with noses seemingly stuck to the ground, but soon they were lifting their heads and going wide on the drift as scent began to evaporate and soon after the line was completely lost. That was a cold and dry day with some sunshine and scent will often evaporate fairly quickly on such a day, especially when there is a dry wind.

Poor scenting days can be most frustrating for both hounds and huntsmen, but such days are soon forgotten when a day of "screaming" scent comes along. Such days are memorable and where hunting is still lawful such days can still be enjoyed on several occasions during an average season. Hounds will fly with a glorious cry on these days, sticking to the line and putting themselves right at the few and far between checks they experience. The hard part on good scenting days is keeping hounds in view, whether mounted or on foot. I remember one such day many years ago when drawing a wide plain at the foot of some high moors and hounds finally pushed a fox out of a large bed of rushes, the fox immediately making for the high moors to the north of the plain. We had a grand view of both fox and hounds and they hunted beautifully straight up the hill pasture and over the wall bordering the high moor, their cry ringing out as they flew up the hill and onto the moorland. Hounds raced over the top and eventually to an old mine working blocked by rocks, where they marked eagerly. I was soon on the spot with the terriers, but old drift mines such as this one were not really places to put a terrier, as they could be incredibly deep, potentially going for more than a mile or two under the hills. Brian Nuttall worked this mine successfully in the 1950s, but this was several decades later, so it was best left, as the terrierman cannot know how much a long-unused mine has deteriorated. Exits could also be a mile or more away and there was also the risk of pockets of poisonous gases lingering in stale air in places, which could be lethal to terriers. Many terriers have been lost in old drift mines and no doubt most have died when encountering such gases, thus this fox was left to run for another day.

I have been hunting with hounds and hunting my own mixed pack, the Blackstone District Ratchers, as well as the Airedale Bloodhounds Foot Pack and the Airedale Beagles, for over forty years now and, generally speaking, I still cannot read scent quality, no matter what the weather. Scent is unpredictable, but so is a hunting day generally, which all adds to the joy of a day spent with hounds amongst our ever-variable and glorious countryside.

25: DEALING WITH RATS:

A northern hunt kennels had been suffering with what seemed like a rat infestation over a few weeks and so Neil Wilson and I arranged to meet there in order to tackle the problem. Not only do rats carry diseases which are lethal to man and beast, but their antics amongst their immediate environment causes much damage to say the least. Add to that the fact that one pair of rats will have as many as thirteen million descendants within three years, if left unchecked and if food supplies are constant enough, and one can see just why we wanted to carry out effective pest control that gets right to the heart of the problem. The hunt staff had tried poisons, but the rats simply refused to eat it, and eight rats had been shot by Jack, the whipper-in, and his friends at night, but a number were still in residence, which left the staff with no other options but to call in the terriers (it is always best to call in the terriers before considering poisons, as working terriers can rid a place of rats in just one visit, with minimal suffering to the rats – a very quick death, compared with hours upon hours of suffering a long lingering death when poisons are used), once the poisons had been removed that is! I say terriers, for a whippet and a small hound were also used that day.

Neil Wilson provided the smoker, a converted strimmer, along with a Jack Russell, Ben, of sixteen years young, and Ted, his working whippet, which has also done well around the shows. I brought along Beck, a veteran worker of fifteen years young which had seen service at far more foxes than she had at rats, and Bracken, a small hound bred by 'Chipper' Smith which has a superb nose and is a great bushing dog, but is also a very keen ratter – hysterically keen I would say. The huntsman, Stephen, assisted operations by carrying out the smoking of the holes, which were mostly in awkward places, but the dogs were keen and quick and we were optimistic.

The holes looked like miniature badger setts, with very well-worn runs, but the first hole was either vacant, or the rats died before they could bolt; gassed very quickly by the exhaust fumes. And so we moved onto a neighbouring warren, which also led into a drain and was not an easy place for the dogs to cover. However, a young rat bolted and Ben had it, then a large doe rat stopped at the entrance and the long snout of Ted the whippet now came in very handy, as he shot into the hole and grabbed the rat before it could back away, shaking it and crushing it very quickly indeed. Anyone who has experience at ratting will know that the combination of shaking and crushing disorientates the rat and then kills it within seconds, making suffering very minimal indeed. That violent shake, in fact, sometimes breaks the neck, making death instantaneous. Another young rat bolted and Ben had that one too, while two more bolted by the drain and got away, as that area could not be covered properly. We then filled the warren with fumes and filled them in, hoping rats would not dig back in.

Bracken marked a small two-holed warren on the top of the bank, close to a skip for the remains of carcasses used to feed hounds, and I was certain this would be a breeding earth. Stephen filled the hole with fumes, but nothing happened, so I asked him to try the other entrance. As soon as he put the pipe in, a large doe rat bolted at speed, but Bracken was on it and ran it down, catching it as it tried to get under the fence at the bottom of the bank, with Beck joining him (she is not as sharp as she used to be!). We then accounted for the litter of young rats. Afterwards, the small pack tried all over this area, but there were no more marks until they tried at a small tin shed where hay was kept for the stables, with Ben and Ted marking in the corner. Neil took Ted outside, while I waited near the side of the shed with Bracken. A large rat bolted at the back and got into a dry-stone wall before Bracken could reach it, with another bolting, but getting back into the hay, while five young rats bolted and were caught by Ted and Ben. The smoker stopped working when we tried to catch up with the rat that got into the wall, and so our tally was eight rats.

They were not easily taken, I can tell you that much, but what we learned that day was, that the kennels were not over-run with rats, which was a relief to the huntsman. I have been back since and checked all over and none of the warrens have been opened up again, so I am hopeful that the rats that were left (only a very small number) have moved on, probably back to the pheasant feeders in the nearby woods, from where they undoubtedly originally came. It hadn't been a spectacular ratting session by any means, but it had been effective. After all, that is all that matters.

26: BRIAN NUTTALL – THE PASSING OF A LEGEND:

Brian Nuttall became a legend in his own lifetime for breeding a strain of working terrier that has produced many incredible workers over several decades, particularly from the late 1950s onwards after Brian began breeding what later became known as the Patterdale terrier. He mated his bitches bred from his grandfather's terrier strain to Breay-bred stock and began producing small, but very strong terriers, which soon made a name for themselves as first rate workers, proving to be great finders and stayers in some of the deepest earths imaginable.

Brian grew up in an area known as the Rossendale Valley and it was and still is an area littered with old mine workings and quarry workings that often hold foxes. Many of these earths cannot be dug and so Brian needed a terrier that could work foxes out of these incredibly deep and dangerous earths, or kill them below should they refuse to bolt, as the moors and dales of the Rossendale Valley where Brian learnt how to hunt and catch foxes are extensively shepherded and foxes can take a heavy toll on lambs during the early spring months (though I have known foxes kill August lambs on occasion). Leaving lamb killing foxes to ground in these vast dens was not an option for Brian, so many of his terriers could finish foxes below ground, but they also had sense enough not to get too badly mauled in the process.

Brian also learnt much from Bert Gripton, with whom he worked terriers from about 1950. He would later meet Cyril Breay and Frank Buck and the abilities of their terriers convinced Brian that these were the right bloodlines to bring into his own developing terrier strain. Breay and Buck were passionate terriermen and they produced some incredible finders, fox bolters and fox killers, from a strain Breay had founded in 1920 and which had been tested in the Pennines, the Yorkshire Dales and the vast borrans of the Lake District, among many other places. Indeed, Breay's strain was largely based on terriers that served with the various fell packs. Brian then produced some of his best terriers and he continued to breed back to Breay bloodlines throughout his life, till very recently when ill health severely limited Brian's breeding scheme.

It wasn't just that Brian bred an incredibly useful terrier strain, it was also that Brian Nuttall was also a very decent and genuine man who always had time to pass on his knowledge when youngsters approached him for advice, and many did. Even experienced terriermen, myself included, sat up and listened when Brian Nuttall spoke, as he was one of the most practical and sensible people I have ever known. Everything he said made sense and his advice worked, simply because it was advice based on practical experience. I wish I had met Brian when I was a youngster just starting with working terriers, as I would have avoided silly mistakes such as entering novice terriers too early. I hunted with Roy Pilling and Baz Unsworth as a lad and we learnt about working terriers together, but often after making mistakes that would have been avoided if I had had someone like Brian to call on for sound, workable advice. Brian

Nuttall wasn't just generous with his advice, but he also lent terriers to those who appreciated their abilities, such as several hunts up and down the country for many, many years, including one or two of the Lakeland fell packs. Scores of gamekeepers also kept, and no doubt still keep, Nuttall bred terriers which they use to help keep fox numbers low on their shoots, which is essential for the protection of wildlife.

I enjoyed many great chats with Brian and we discovered that he had hunted many of the areas I have hunted over the years, even having terriers trapped in the same earths, only about thirty years apart. His passing is a sad blow to the hunting world generally, but particularly the world of the working terrier. He will be sadly missed. Condolences to his family.

27: RATTING MEMORIES:

I have had some great days hunting rats and one of the best places and most fruitful of places it has to be said, was the River Roch, which, during the 1970s and 1980s, was polluted enough for rats to proliferate. Some of the banks were rather steep and it was hair-raising to have rats flying out of holes at terrific speeds and shooting past your ears as they jumped for the river, the terriers unable to get many of them. Some of the spots were on more level ground, however, and our team of terriers, lurchers and even an occasional ex-track racing greyhound, became rather adept at dodging through the undergrowth and low-growing branches of willows in order to catch their rats before they reached the safety of the river, where they would inevitably dive straight under the water and make for the opposite bank. Occasionally the terriers would catch one in the water or the lurchers caught a rat as it emerged in order to cross some shingle, or sandbank, but mostly they found safety in the water, unless Roy, my hunting partner for many years, had his .410 shotgun at the ready.

I remember one rat hole under some willows being a particularly difficult spot, as it was close to the river and rats had only a short distance to run, yet we took many rats from this place, the terriers agility on display as they bobbed and weaved among the low-lying branches of the willows and snapped up many a rat before it could get into the river. If I remember correctly, even my greyhound, Bess, caught a few rats that bolted from this warren and many a Sunday morning found us ratting along this stretch of river, which is in the industrial heartland a few miles north of Manchester.

Another great memory was when we were ratting down in Cheshire just after the shooting season had ended and Turk caught probably the biggest rat I have ever seen. We were ratting in a corn field and the rats had been helping themselves to the crop, and many were growing to huge sizes on such a rich and easily accessible diet. A rat bolted from a hole towards the edge of the field lying close to the farm outbuildings and it was massively fat, yet could still move at terrific speed, but Turk was on it and he ran it down just before it reached a barn full of bales, where it would have been safe. I did photograph this large rat, but have since lost the photos.

 Farmyards have always been great places to rat and one, in the hills above Bury in East Lancashire, was holding quite a good sized population of rats. Turk caught a huge doe rat that bolted from a hole we smoked that was situated in the dung heap, just before it got into a nearby stable. We ratted all around this farmyard and took well over a dozen rats from various locations, but before we started, I had asked the farmer to lock her cats up while we ratted. I always break my terriers to cats, but in the heat of a ratting session anything could have happened, so it seemed better to be safe than sorry. Those few rats that did escape our team of terriers took shelter in the shed which housed the cats and the farmer later found their carcasses lying in among her beloved pets. That was one of the most satisfying ratting sessions I have ever taken part in, simply because almost every rat was accounted for and the farmer had no more problems with them after that one visit, which demonstrates just how effective ratting with terriers can be when carrying out necessary pest control.

 Another great session in and around a farmyard was in Nottingham with Carl Noon, who had the brother to my two terriers Turk and Beck; a dog named Flint which was a cracking little worker. One of the rats popped its head out and tried to go back, but Turk stuck his long snout into the hole and managed to get hold of it, pulling it out of the warren and killing it quickly, though it did manage to bite him a time or two before he killed it. Another big rat shot out and ran down the side of a nearby shed, but again Turk had it before it could reach safety. That too, was one of the biggest rats I have ever taken. Turk was particularly quick and agile and he caught many rats, but all of my terriers have been great little ratters and Pep, my Jack Russell, was a little cracker. She could mark rat holes with unerring accuracy, which saved a lot of time, as in those days I mostly ferreted rats, but in more recent years have used a converted strimmer for smoking them out, which has proven to be most effective and is a quicker process than ferreting.

 I remember the first rat I ever took. I had taken on an ex-track racing greyhound named Bess and was in the process of getting her fit and ready for the coming season (Bess made a good ferreting dog and was most useful on the lamp too, even retrieving rabbits, which was rare for a greyhound). I had taken her on a long walk into the hills and as I was heading for home I spotted something in the grass, on the edge of a field bordering a number of allotments. It was a large rat drinking from a small pool of water that had gathered in a cow's hoof print in the ground, after the rain earlier that day. Bess was away as soon as she saw it and the rat ran for the allotments, from where it had obviously come, but it didn't make it. Bess had it very quickly and killed it with a quick shake and a crushing bite, but not before it bit her quite badly on the muzzle, leaving a permanent scar as a reminder of that day.

I had many a good day walking along my local brook which in days past was quite polluted and held a good few rats. One spot, by a little bridge close to a farm where I often worked as a young lad, held a lot of rats over the years. This was a pile of riverbed stones and the rats seemed to love sheltering in them. I often put a ferret in after the terriers had marked, and rats would bolt and head straight for the brook. This brook was mostly shallow, so the terriers often took the rats even when they reached the water. In fact, they were so efficient at quickly snatching up rats that, after a few years of occasionally ratting along this waterway, rats no longer lived along its banks. That was a good thing, as a housing estate was nearby and public health was protected when rats abandoned an area. As I said at the beginning, I have enjoyed many great ratting sessions, which, I suppose, are mostly too numerous to recount.

28: TAMING THE TROUBLESOME TERRIER:

Terriers have been bred to be fiery when roused simply because they have been required to face large, hard-biting quarry for centuries – quarry that is often larger and fiercer than themselves. This means that our working terriers are incredibly game, making them most useful when it comes to the control of predators that can take a heavy toll on livestock, but unfortunately that gameness, that fiery disposition when roused, can sometimes overspill into everyday life and problems are the inevitable result.

Terriers can be bad fighters for instance, or they may take to chewing furniture and other household objects which don't come cheap. Kennelling terriers may be the best option for some, though cages, or crates to use the more politically 'correct' phrase, can be used to confine terriers so that they do not ruin expensive goods, or fight when no-one is around to prevent them from doing so. I have to say that occasionally two terriers can take a severe dislike to one another for whatever reason, possibly a fall-out over a bit of food, or perhaps whilst marking a rat hole, and very often all one can do in such a situation is to keep them separated, though very often such terriers will work well together and exercise well together, but they cannot tolerate one another within the close confines of a kennel or a house. Willie Irving of the Melbreak Foxhounds had two terriers during the 1930s, Jerry and Rock, both of which feature in his famous Crummock Water photograph taken in 1936, which got on well when out with hounds, provided they were on separate couplings, but which fought fiercely when back at the kennels, so Willie simply had to keep them separated in such situations and he made certain that they never got to ground together, for obvious reasons. Cyril Breay's Rusty developed a loathing for his own sire, Bingo, and this pair of terriers had to be kept separate at all times. When two terriers develop such a hatred of each other, fights are usually to the death if no intervention occurs. However, some seem to fight just for the sake of it.

At Lowther Show Eddie Pool was telling me about his famous terrier Trim and Bill Crisp's equally famous Mischief. They fought every time they met, but afterwards would always be the best of pals and got on as though nothing had happened – as if such fights were just a game they played together. Both of these terriers became legendary workers with the Ullswater Foxhounds during the 1960s and they are still talked about today, but such fights are different to a troublesome sort of terrier that wants to fight every dog it comes across. Such a disposition is very troublesome to the owner and is often a result of the terrier having been mauled by a dog when a puppy, though sometimes they are quarrelsome simply because of boredom. If a terrier has a strong working instinct that is not utilised, problems often result.

Regular exercise periods and allowing your terrier to work, legally of course, will help tremendously with behavioural problems, though sometimes more needs to be done. A terrier that fights will set its mind on such a course, so it is essential that the owner acts quickly to change the thought processes of a troublesome tyke. Jerking the lead back while telling your terrier to "leave it" is one way to distract the thoughts, as is throwing a set of keys on the ground next to the terrier – something some dog behavioural therapists recommend – though I have found that cracking a leather leash on the ground in front of the terrier, then jerking the lead back and commanding it to "leave" is much more effective, whilst also turning the terrier away from the dog that is the subject of such aggression. Interrupting the thought processes and distracting them is a very effective way of switching off aggressive behaviour, but other methods will be necessary when it comes to the more troublesome terriers.

If a working terrier, or any dog for that matter, feels secure and content, then their behaviour improves. For a dog to feel secure and content it must know its place in the pack – that is, in the family, which the dog will view as its pack. It is vital, and this cannot be stressed enough, that a terrier is subject to all in the family, including children if there are any. If you keep your terrier in the home, then have a certain area where it sleeps. Some enjoy having their dogs on their knee, allowing them on the furniture, but do not allow this all the time. More importantly, only allow your terrier on your knee when you say so. Never allow it to lie above you, say on the back of the sofa, for a commanding position will give your terrier ambitions to be pack leader and that can lead to problems, including the biting of children. Never allow your terrier to jump on the furniture and push off your child, or even yourself, taking your place, as that will give them ideas far above their station. In fact, if a terrier behaves in this way, trying to push you off the furniture, or trying to take your place, then it is already attempting to be the "boss" of your household. Telling your dog to go to its bed for much of the time and not allowing it on the furniture whenever it feels like it, is vital for a well-balanced and well-behaved terrier that feels secure in its role in the family. Another tip is not to allow it to go through doors or gates before you when not in a working environment. This tells your dog that you are pack leader and this in turn will aid subjection.

Another tip is to make certain that your terrier carries out your commands. Also, never reward bad behaviour with praise or treats. For instance, some dogs are frightened by fireworks and many owners comfort their dog, stroking and caressing them. This is actually rewarding the dog for such behaviour and it only serves to make them worse. Putting such a dog in a cage and covering the cage with a sheet, or towels will help the dog to feel more secure. Do not even talk to a dog that behaves in such a way, just provide a safe, secure enclosed environment and leave it well alone. I have done this with my own terriers on bonfire night over the years and many of them become far less bothered by fireworks over time. Having them on your knee and cuddling them simply makes them worse, reinforcing bad behaviour.

Many will say that bad behaviour can be corrected by castrating a dog terrier or spaying a bitch, if all other methods fail. There are no guarantees, however, that this course of action will work. Firm and consistent discipline is always the best option when dealing with problem dogs.

Firm commands and showing your disfavour in no uncertain terms is essential when commands are not carried out, or when bad behaviour rears its ugly head. Dogs are like children in many ways – spoil them and they become unpleasant company. Dogs should not be pack leader, just as children should not rule their parents. Be firm and discipline your terrier when it is necessary to do so, distract thoughts and administer discipline when behaving badly, while keeping your terrier in its proper place within the household. All of this, together with good food, a warm, dry bed and plenty of affection and praise when appropriate, will do much to produce a terrier that is a pleasure, not a liability, to own.

29: MONTY – CORNERSTONE OF THE JOHN PARK STRAIN:

John Park's Monty was bred by John Whaley of Mallerstang out of his bitch, Trixie, a bitch that greatly impressed Cyril Breay, and Breay's Rusty, the son of Bingo and a famous worker to fox which saw service with at least two packs of foxhounds. John Whaley kept the Breay strain of terrier and he greatly respected, even revered, the great Cyril Breay throughout his lifetime. Whaley bred some incredible workers from his Breay strain terriers and Monty must be considered as one of the very best.

Monty was bred under the guidance of Mister Breay and he was originally passed on to Frank Buck, who gave him to a lady living in the same village as Frank; a small hillside village called Harmby, which is a stone's throw away from Leyburn in Wensleydale. Sadly though, the lady died soon afterwards and so Monty was returned to Frank Buck. It was from Frank that John Park obtained this terrier. John had been keeping and working terriers for a few years by this time, keeping a mix of Jack Russell terriers and fell type terriers, but it was Monty who really began the John Park strain of working terrier, which is now so famous among terriermen in many different countries.

Monty was born in the 1960s when badger digging, carried out properly by knowledgeable terriermen who dealt with quarry as humanely as possible, was still considered an effective and legitimate form of pest control, and it was at badger that Monty excelled. John was called out to deal with a badger that was killing livestock at a farm near Malton in North Yorkshire and he took Monty along to a three hundred acre field with two well-run holes right in the middle of it.

Monty was entered and he could soon be heard baying at a depth of around three feet or so. Monty had a loud, booming voice at quarry and this aided the diggers in the days before electronic locators came on the scene. This meant that terriermen of those days had to employ fieldcraft whilst carrying out terrier work and John Park soon became expert at locating his terriers as they worked busily below ground. John began digging and he said that it was like trying to dig up a road, the earth was that hard and impacted, the soil soon giving way to chalk and flint.

After an age of hard digging John broke through to Monty, who was working an albino badger. John attempted to tail it, but it charged Monty out of the way and disappeared deeper into the sett. Monty went deeper too and what followed was a hard twelve hour dig that finally saw John break through at eleven o'clock that night, uncovering Monty and the five badgers the terrier had bottled-up. However, the albino badger was not among them and so John had to give it best after such an exhaustingly long dig. Monty proved to be an incredible stayer to fox or badger and John stated that Monty would rather have died than leave his quarry. It is no wonder then that Monty became the cornerstone of the John Park strain, which sired some incredible workers, the most noteworthy being Park's Bingo, named in honour of Mister Breay's famous worker that was also the grandsire of Monty.

Harry Hines, a farmer who lived and farmed near John Park, owned a bitch named Brandy that was out of the last litter of puppies sired by Harry Hardisty's Turk. Harry Hines went to school with Harry Hardisty and was a close friend, so it isn't surprising that he owned a bitch out of Hardisty's Turk. John Park put Monty to the Turk-bred Brandy and produced an outstanding litter, the best of which was Park's Bingo. As incredible at work as Monty was, Bingo was an even better worker and he became the best and most reliable terrier that John Park has ever owned, and that is saying something, for, as John Moore said, Park had a kennel full of superb workers for many, many years, all of which were completely reliable.

On more than one occasion Bingo found foxes or badgers in places that had already been dug, being full of human, dog and quarry scent, where other terriers had indicated there was nothing else at home. During one dig two terriers were tried at the end of it and they showed no further interest, yet Bingo was keen to go, so John loosed him. John then dug to his terrier and accounted for a fox and a badger. It is interesting to note that many of Cyril Breay's strain of terrier were capable of such feats and David Machin's Breay-bred terriers, particularly Moley and Whisky, could find more fox or badger in a badly foiled earth after other terriers had failed to find anything.

John Park rates finding very highly and both Monty and Bingo, and consequently many others from Park's strain, were exceptional finders, not to mention great stayers. John Park has taken part in many long digs over the years and it was nothing unusual for his terriers to stay with quarry for anywhere upwards of seventeen hours or more. In fact, Park, as well as any good terrierman come to that, would not waste kennel room on any terrier that wasn't a reliable finder and stayer.

John Park based his further breeding on Bingo after he became an utterly dependable worker and this breeding soon became popular in several different countries. There is quite a lot of Park breeding in Ireland today, as well as in America, where terrier work isn't restricted. But even in the British Isles where the law restricts terrier work to some extent, it is still possible to breed and use working terriers and some today are still finding the John Park strain to be very useful indeed. This is not surprising, given the background of this strain, which is based on excellent working stock that was tested in some of the worst places imaginable.

30: WORKING TERRIER RESCUES:

The first rescue was unusual in that no terrier was to ground. January 1936 saw the Blencathra Foxhounds rousing a fox after a meet at Mungrisedale, scene of countless top class hunts with this famous pack, which then gave them a long hunt, starting at 10.15am and concluding at 4.20pm. Reynard, often called 'Jacky' by Lakeland hunters in those days, covered miles that day, taking hounds over the rough fells at Mungrisedale, over Carrock, on towards and over Saddleback (the alternative name for the Blencathra Mountain), across Greystoke Park, before heading back to the Mungrisedale area, where Reynard was accounted for, being caught in a beck. The terriers joined in and Douglas Paisley was forced to wade into the icy cold mountain waters in order to prevent the terriers from drowning. While this hunt was going on four hounds got away on another fox over Swinside Breast, Mosedale, over Caldew and Bowscale Fell, before they pulled him down in the village.

In March 1925 the Ullswater Foxhounds met at Deepdale Hall, but didn't find a fox until drawing the infamous Dove Crag; scene of many a hound or terrier rescue and unfortunately a place where many a hound and not a few terriers have fallen to their deaths while trying to flush a 'binked' fox. This fox was roused safely from Dove Crag and a fast hunt followed, taking the pack to Rydal, Hogarth Ghyll, round Dodd End and to ground at

Rowantree Knott. Braithwaite Wilson, in his first season as huntsman after taking over from 'Auld Hunty,' Joe Bowman, entered two terriers on arriving at the scene, and as was common in those days they killed their fox to ground, before it became obvious the two terriers were in trouble. With darkness coming on they were forced to leave the terriers in, but were back at first light the next day, with digging going on all day. In the worst places dynamite was often used to break big rocks so they could be moved out of the way; a common practise long before Frank Buck became noted for the use of dynamite during terrier rescues, but this report does not state if such tactics were employed during this rescue, but what it does tell us is that this was a long, hard dig and that it was an all day job before terriers and dead fox were finally pulled out that night.

Having mentioned the dynamiting of trapped terriers, a skill brought to fell hunting by quarrymen who were experts at blasting immoveable rocks, in February 1918 the Eskdale and Ennerdale Foxhounds, hunted at that time by Willie Porter, noted as both a great houndsman and terrierman whose memory is still highly regarded to this day, ran a fox into a fissure at a crag on Brotherilkeld Fell. Merry was sent to bolt it, but the terrier worried the fox in and was trapped during the encounter. What followed was one of the hardest digs the Lakes has ever witnessed, lasting a long, tiring, hard eight days until finally Merry was rescued, with dynamite having to be used in order to shift large rocks hampering progress. The terrier had eaten most of the fox by the time the diggers finally broke through.

Our next terrier rescue involved the Blencathra Foxhounds once again, with a fox being run into what proved to be an old mineshaft, on the eastern flank of the Blencathra range above Mungrisedale. This hunt took place in March 1953 when Johnny Richardson was in the early years of a long career as huntsman. Tess and Betty were sent in after the fox and while tackling it the fox and two terriers fell at least 80ft into the old shaft. Johnny Richardson was lowered 180ft to a ledge, together with his whipper-in, Anthony Chapman, and two shepherds, Jack Bland, the father of Richard 'Pritch' Bland, and Bill Waite, but Johnny went on alone, wearing a metal helmet to protect him from rock falls. Betty was alright, but poor Tess, walked I believe by Jack Bland at High Lodore Farm, Borrowdale, had broken her leg in the fall. The fox was dead. The terriers and dead fox were brought out in a sack and no doubt there were some hearty celebrations that night.

In September 1948 hounds ran a fox to ground during a Tickham hunt and Tom Kirkby was asked to put in his terrier, Tinker. This was during what was then known as cub-hunting time and so hounds were out early and the fox was run in early on that Monday morning too. Tinker was two years old at the time and it was soon obvious the terrier was in trouble, so digging started that same day and the going soon became very hard indeed, as underneath the turf and soil was hard chalk rock, which basically had to be chipped away. Over the next three days a twelve-foot trench was dug and after a hard slog by the digging team, Tinker was finally reached and lifted from that earth. It had taken three hard days of digging, but all agreed the effort had been very worthwhile. Tinker was given warm milk and brandy, then wrapped in a blanket and the terrier was soon perking-up.

In April 1966 Michael Rollinson of Bacup in Lancashire headed to Staffordshire on a rabbiting trip and his terriers, Frisky and Smut, got to ground in a fox hole and failed to return. This was on the Sunday morning. It wasn't long before they started digging and continued till the early hours of Monday morning, when they deemed it best to take some rest. On returning they could hear one of the terriers whining and so began digging eagerly. Anyone who has been involved in terrier rescues will know how uplifting and motivating it is when the sound of a terrier is heard, especially if the earth has mostly been silent. It gives renewed strength and energy to the team of diggers. That is what happened that Monday upon their return. They then dug up tons of earth and after 70hours to ground they finally broke through and could see Frisky's nose poking through a small hole. Upon clearing this Frisky was freed, but poor smut was lay dead closeby. The account doesn't explain what killed Smut, but my guess is suffocation, there not being enough air in that place for two terriers.

In April 1928 author and Novelist Hugh Walpole's cocker spaniel got into an old abandoned mine at Brandelhow above Derwentwater and Tom Pepper, a Keswick labourer, was called in to help. He put in his terrier and the spaniel later found its way out, but the terrier failed to emerge and was in for a week before pepper located his dog, at the bottom of a 100ft shaft on the fellside. Pepper was lowered down on a rope and was then lifted out with his game terrier, which had undoubtedly been side-tracked by foxes upon entering that old mine. I wonder if Tom Pepper was related to Jack and Frank Pepper of Bowderstone?

On the eastern fells above Ullswater, twixt Pooley Bridge and Patterdale, hounds ran a fox to earth on Swarthfell, 1800ft high on the fellside. The fox was bolted by a terrier and it then jumped 60ft down a precipice, making off, but being caught soon after by hounds. On emerging, the terrier got a little over-excited, as terriers do, and tried to follow the fox, but became trapped on a crag ledge whilst doing so. One of the regular followers was lowered down on ropes and the terrier was brought to safety, but in the process of rescuing the terrier a boulder was dislodged and it struck one of the hounds, killing it. There have been many tragedies on the fells of the Lake District, involving people, hounds and terriers. This occurred in April 1926 when Braithwaite Wilson was huntsman, having taken over from Joe Bowman just two years before.

31: WORKING TERRIERS – PREVENTING TROUBLESOME TENDENCIES:

In a previous chapter discussing dealing with troublesome terriers, I stated that such troubles often result from the fact that terriers are bred to be fiery and strong-willed, which makes some resist discipline and attempt to become "pack" leader if given even the slightest opportunity. However, there is much that can be done in order to prevent troublesome tendencies from developing in the first place. The very first step is to either purchase a puppy, preferably at eight weeks of age – a good age to begin moulding a terrier into a well-behaved working dog, or breed your own, which can be most rewarding. If choosing to breed your own, breed only from a dog and bitch terrier that are proven workers and that are not troublesome.

Adult terriers can be trained when using firm, consistent discipline, together with patient handling, but the training and shaping of a puppy is always going to be the best and easiest option for those who wish to work terriers. Of course, methods vary a little with each breed of working terrier, not to mention each individual dog or bitch, as some are easier to train and handle than others. Lakeland terriers generally are often fiery, bold and fearless and one must be strong in providing consistent and firm discipline, as they can be terribly headstrong. On the other hand, Border terriers and fell terriers with quite an influence of Border terrier blood, can often be more docile, even sensitive, so handling them more gently is necessary, as one does not want to break the spirit of any dog when training and assisting the terrier to know its proper place in the family arrangement. Of course, not all Border terriers are sensitive, just as not all Lakeland terriers are fiery and very headstrong. Take Colin Armstrong's excellent working Border terrier, Bragg, as an example.

Colin breeds a very game and typey strain of unregistered Lakeland terrier based mostly on John Cowen's bloodlines, but he has also owned and worked other breeds, such as Jack Russells and an occasional Border terrier. Bragg was bred by Joe Dobinson, one-time terrierman to the Zetland Foxhounds, and Colin first tried him at fox when he was just seven and a-half months of age, which wasn't his usual practice it has to be noted. Unlike many Border terriers, Bragg was bold and fearless and when a fox was run into a large stickpile Bragg was eager to go, so Joe asked Colin to try him. Bragg went eagerly and quickly bolted the first fox, failing to re-emerge. Colin and Joe dug into the stickpile and sometime later uncovered the young Bragg and the now dead fox. A stint at fox at such a young age would ruin most Border terriers, but Bragg was not of a sensitive nature, which was true of many of Joe Dobinson's excellent strain, and Joe deemed the terrier ready to go, as he knew his strain inside-out.

Bragg went from strength to strength after this and he became a great finder. The Melbreak Foxhounds had run a fox into a drain near Loweswater at a place where three drains meet. Three hunt terriers were tried, but all failed to find the fox, the running water pouring out of the drains undoubtedly affecting scent quality in the earth. However, Bragg tried all three entrances and shot up the middle drain, finding his fox after a struggle through the water.

Getting back to preventing troublesome tendencies, it is important to deal with each individual terrier according to its own personality, though firm and consistent discipline is always going to be essential, no matter whether a terrier be bold, or of a quieter, more retiring disposition, as a working terrier must know that you are the dominant "pack" member. One way to instil such a lesson from very early on is to approach and play with your puppy, or even carry out short basic training sessions such as "sit" and "lie-down" while it is on its bed. A terrier, or any breed of dog come to that, must accept that its owner has the right to "invade" its space without any aggression whatsoever in response to this. Dogs have a strong sense of territory, yet all pack members can roam in that territory without being mauled. It is the same in the family. A dog will view the home and garden, or even areas where regular exercise is carried out, as the "packs" territory, accepting that all members of the "pack" can roam freely there. That is how it should be. Some dogs, or, that is, dogs which are allowed to rule the roost so to speak, can become aggressive and even take to biting their owners or children in the family, when they feel that their space is being invaded. This can even be a place on the furniture. I have seen dogs growling and snapping at their owners when they tried to sit on the sofa. This is simply because such dogs have become "boss" of their owners, ruling the home and taking the prominent places as their own.

Getting a puppy familiar with your presence and each member of the family's presence in areas where it sleeps and even eats will ensure that your working terrier grows to know its proper place. Any owner of a dog should be able to take food from it without even a slight sign of aggression, though I am not saying that you should practise such a thing, nor am I recommending that you try this. Allow your terrier to eat in peace, as this will aid it to settle into the family and to be content. But do go to it and stroke and play and even carry out a little training while it is on its bed, with each member of the family doing the same on a regular basis as the puppy grows. This will help your terrier know its proper place – subject to the family.

Carry out regular, but short training sessions, making certain commands are obeyed, and get your children joining in whenever possible. One of the most important lessons to instil early on is the "come" command. Use the puppy's name and command it to "come" or "come-on" in a kind, enthusiastic, even fun, voice. It is good to use treats such as milk drops as a reward when the puppy comes to you, while also praising and playing a little with the puppy, making training sessions fun. Sit, lie-down and stay are also important lessons to instil, as is lead training. When you carry out such training sessions in a fun, yet firm, way, instilling vital lessons, you again help a dog to know its proper place. Knowing its proper place will thus ensure that a puppy thrives and feels safe and content, for aggression and bad tendencies are usually a result of a dog failing to feel safe, secure and content. Dogs which feel threatened and unsettled can become aggressive and problematic and if your puppy is "top" dog in your home, it will grow to defend that position, feeling threatened by rivals, even human rivals, so keep it in its proper place from day one and problems should then be very few and far between. Even if you choose to purchase adult terriers and problematic behaviour arises, then the same principles apply.

32: OBTAINING PERMISSION TO WORK TERRIERS:

Obtaining permission to work your terriers is not easy these days, and is perhaps a little more difficult in England and Wales ever since the hunting ban was implemented back in 2005. Difficult it may be, but it is not impossible and I would like to pass on a few tips which have helped me obtain a lot of permission over the years.

A respectful attitude towards farmers and gamekeepers and other landowners is essential. If you approach any landowner with an attitude, then kiss goodbye to obtaining any kind of permission. I have always got on well with farmers, but few of them will suffer fools gladly and approaching them in any way other than a respectful one will fail miserably. Being respectful simply means that on approaching a landowner one must be polite and well mannered. Introduce yourself with your full name and get straight to the point, asking if they would please allow you over their land in order to provide a free pest control service, while at the same time getting the message across that you will work within the law. A respectful attitude will also mean that you will not turn up at a farm or any other location dressed scruffily. I have found it most effective to be smartly dressed with a shirt and tie, jacket and trousers, avoiding jeans and other casual wear, which can give a wrong impression. Be respectful and dress smartly; those are the first two things to keep in mind when seeking permission.

It is also important to stress that you will show proper due respect for the land over which you hunt. Inform the landowner that you will close gates after use and that you will keep out of fields full of livestock such as sheep and cattle. Stress that your dogs are fully broken to all forms of farm livestock and if the farmer or gamekeeper wishes for you to keep your dogs on a lead between the places where you will use them, then cheerfully agree to do so. If you have to go over fences or stone walls, make certain that you do no damage, but should you knock a stone or two off a wall top, then replace them neatly and carefully immediately. Do not think to yourself that you will replace the stones on the way back, as you may end up taking a different route and that would then mean that the stones would be left loose on the ground.

A wall without a proper top to it is weakened and will begin to deteriorate, so be diligent in making immediate repairs, if and when you damage a wall or even a fence. I have sometimes gone beyond this and made small repairs, which damage I hadn't caused. A wall without a few top stones will encourage sheep to jump over and this will weaken the wall further, so make certain, as I have said, that such stones are very quickly replaced, even if you haven't knocked them off. In fact, upon asking for permission, it is good to mention to a farmer that if you see any damage to a fence or wall, you will repair it, or, if that isn't possible, you will let him know about it upon your return to the farm at the end of the day. Also, let the landowner know that if you see any of his livestock in any kind of trouble, you will inform him immediately. I have done such things on several occasions, once when a sheep was stuck in a bog and John Hill and I lifted it out, but it was so weakened it could not get up, so I fetched the farmer immediately. Another sheep was stuck in the cleft of a crag and I got it free and to safety, but its back leg was damaged and it couldn't walk. Again, I fetched the farmer immediately. On another occasion a bullock was trapped in a ditch and I informed the farmer straight away. Such actions have helped me keep permission that I have now had for decades, so it is well worth the effort.

Let the farmer or keeper know that you will remove any rats that may settle around his homestead and outbuildings. This offer may well secure your permission, though a landowner will likely be glad of your services regarding any kind of pest, such as foxes and mink, or even moles if you know how to trap them.

Stressing how well behaved and well trained your dogs are is also important, as no landowner wishes to have uncontrollable dogs on the loose around livestock. Sound basic training and diligent stock breaking must be carried out before hunting your charges. This is vital if you are to obtain and keep any permission you seek. Having written permission is essential these days and the law requires it in some countries, so make out a neatly prepared form which states that you offer a free pest control service which will be carried out within the law and have two copies for the farmer to sign and date. He can keep one and you keep the other, making certain you also leave him with your telephone number and address if the landowner requires this. Being open in such a way shows that you have nothing to hide and that you are not up to any kind of criminal activity.

Having succeeded in obtaining permission, one must then keep it and that is easily done by demonstrating what you have promised, respect for land and livestock. Being polite and friendly and spending a bit of time chatting to the farmer when opportunity arises will also help. Some have volunteered to assist the landowner without charge during very busy periods and this has greatly assisted in them keeping in the landowner's good books for many years. Good land to hunt over is a treasure and one must do everything possible to obtain and keep such land.

33: WHEN TO BREED FROM WORKING TERRIERS:

A subject that has been the cause of some controversy over the years is when to breed from working terriers, dogs and bitches. We all have our own way of doing things of course and there can be no hard rules to follow in such matters, just as entering methods and preferences for coat type differ among even experienced and knowledgeable terriermen, but a few common-sense guidelines are surely not out of place, as novice terriermen are slowly building their knowledge through experience and hopefully the advice of those such as myself who are now a little long in the tooth, looking back on far more years of working terriers than those to come, will be of some value.

There may be those who believe that as soon as a bitch begins coming in-season and a dog terrier is capable of fathering puppies it must be ready to breed from, as nature has endowed them with that ability at only a few months of age, but such reasoning is very unsound. This is firstly because both dog and bitch terriers do not stop developing until they reach the age of eighteen months, when bone structure and muscle will finally stop growing. The structure of the jaw and teeth do not stop fully developing until this age too and that is why many very good and experienced terriermen elect to refrain from entering a terrier to large quarry until they reach the age of eighteen months. There have been exceptions to this of course, such as a son of W.H. Cliff's famous terrier, Hemp, which by 1890 had carved out a great reputation as a worker. The son of Hemp entered to otter at just 6 months of age and closed with his quarry, hanging onto it in spite of the otter retaliating and the icy cold water in which the encounter took place. The other four terriers coming to the youngster's aid and killing the otter. The account goes on to state that 4 of the 5 terriers out that day were of the old Cumberland Hill strain (the original Patterdale terrier) bred by G.M. Nelson of Keswick, these bloodlines being founded on Lord Beresford's strain of terrier famous for their game qualities at organised badger digs. It is interesting to note that the Ullswater terriers were founded on these same bloodlines. Of course, entering to large quarry at just 6 months is not recommended.

Secondly, an immature terrier should not be bred from at too young an age simply because a bitch is not ready to settle down with a litter of puppies. Indeed, when they first come into season at the age of six to eight months, bitches are far too immature mentally and emotionally for having and rearing puppies. An immature bitch is simply not ready for having a litter of puppies and by the time of the second season, at around twelve months of age (heats vary amongst bitches and some may not have their first season until they are twelve months of age) I would say the same is true. It is fair to say that a dog or bitch terrier will be more mature by the age of twelve months, physically, mentally and emotionally, but the fact remains that they are not fully mature.

The third reason, and probably the most important reason from a terrierman's perspective, for not breeding from immature terriers is that they are lacking work experience. If you wish to pass on good working qualities to the next generation of working terriers, then both the sire and the dam must have plenty of experience at work. This is because working qualities are passed on through the genes of the dog and bitch, but how can such qualities be passed on if the sire and dam lack such experience at work?

To breed from what are essentially non-workers at the age of twelve months (even if you have entered your terriers to large quarry at such an age they will still be lacking vital experience) is to risk producing either a weakened working instinct or even a non-working instinct in future generations, which is undesirable to say the least. If you disagree with this, and you are entitled to do so of course, just take a look at most pedigree breeds of once working terriers, which now produce mostly useless stock simply because they are bred from non-workers.

A fourth reason for not breeding from less mature stock is because they have not been given a chance to prove themselves workers. A terrier can only develop desirable qualities such as finding, working up to large quarry such as foxes so that they will bolt, or stay to a fox that won't bolt, if it is given regular work over a period of time. This period of time should be for at least one season, though my personal preference is to breed only from dogs or bitches that have proven themselves good and reliable workers over at least two seasons. This means that those desirable qualities that have been developed over time can be passed on to the next generation which, given time and opportunity, will also develop into good, if not great, workers. Take my terrier, Ghyll, as an example.

Ghyll went to earth on his first fox at around fourteen or fifteen months of age, which is about the age that I like to give a novice terrier its first stint to ground at large quarry. He went to his fox and bayed at it, but he wouldn't stay and came off soon after. I left him alone while I dug to another terrier, making no fuss at all and leaving him to it. Not long after, he went to earth on his own and, after staying with his fox while I dug, baying and working it hard, he killed it below, just as I was breaking through. Ghyll never looked back after that and he became an incredible worker – a finder, a stayer and a terrier which finished his foxes without being mauled by them. Ghyll was bred down from Breay/Buck stock through John Park breeding, Tony Broadbent's legendary worker, Boozer. Sadly, Ghyll was run over and killed by a car during his fifth season, before I had put him onto my bitch, Mist, who was still developing as a worker. I do not doubt the quality of that intended litter, as both Ghyll and Mist were bred from a long line of workers and so they would have produced good, if not great, workers, but only if given a chance to fully mature physically, mentally and emotionally, as well as being given a chance to develop into experienced and thus proven workers. I did get a litter from Mist eventually, once she had proven herself, when put to Fell, another cracking worker bred by Wendy Pinkney, all of the litter maturing into excellent workers, Turk being an exceptionally good worker.

It is both common-sense and good practice to be patient and wait before breeding from either a dog or bitch terrier, so that they can be given a chance to pass on their desirable qualities after proving themselves good workers. As Del Boy would say, "you know it makes sense."

34: THE FOUNDATION STOCK OF MODERN WORKING FELL, LAKELAND & PATTERDALE TERRIERS:

Old newspaper accounts give us some insight into the foundation stock of modern strains of fell, Lakeland and Patterdale terriers and one thing is clear from such sources – that these terriers of former centuries were incredibly game and hardy workers which have passed on such qualities with each successive generation.

Towards the end of July 1892 an otter was spotted at Spooney Beck near the River Greta and passing was Joe Martin of Keswick with his terrier, Bill, a noted worker of the time. Bill was put in a drain where the otter had crept in and was soon hard at it, but after an hour Bill was exhausted and had taken quite a bit of punishment, as otters are a hard biting quarry. A Mister Longrigg turned up with yet another noted terrier of the time, Lady, and she joined Bill in the fray and the two of them killed the otter after a further 30 minutes to ground. Lady and Bill were both fox terriers which served with the Blencathra Foxhounds and had proven themselves superb workers, which is evident from this account that appeared in the Cumberland and Westmorland Herald on Saturday July 30th 1892. It is interesting to note that Jim Dalton's strain of fell terrier were party bred from fox terriers, as were Douglas Paisley's Lakeland terrier strain, which means it is entirely possible that Bill or Lady, perhaps both of these game fox terriers, featured in the foundation stock of their strains. Dalton began hunting the Blencathra Foxhounds in 1894, hunting with them before this time, so he would have known both of these terriers and would have seen them at work. Paisley began breeding fell terriers, the typey improved terrier that became known as the Lakeland terrier in 1921, in 1900 and so it is reasonable to assume that Paisley used Dalton stud dogs on his bitches, which also may have been Blencathra bred, his foundation bitch being Wasp.

Dan Pattinson of the Ullswater Foxhounds bred and worked some incredibly game stock and Jack was one of his best. After a meet at

Hartsopp Hall in the February of 1867, hounds struck a drag in the lower pastures, which took them over the Kirkstone fells and to the head of the glorious Troutbeck Valley, where Beatrix Potter once farmed; occasionally watching the Coniston Foxhounds hunting through the valley as she tended her flock of hardy herdwick sheep. Hounds dragged to Swine Crag and then on to Broad How Borran, which, even then, had a reputation as a notoriously bad place from where it was usually impossible to bolt foxes. Pattinson, the huntsman, had three terriers by his side, these being Crab, Banter and Jack, with Jack being selected to have a go at this bad place, but with few, if any, expectations of a successful outcome.

Jack disappeared into the vast and seemingly bottomless Broad How Borran and, knowing how bad this place is, with terriers having been lost here over the years and countless foxes having been given best here because the terriers could either not find them, or they couldn't reach them in order to effect a bolt, Dan Pattinson's heart must have been in his mouth, so to speak, when he saw his little faithful tyke disappearing into this rocky fortress where 'Jacky' (an ancient Lakeland name for a fox which seems to have originated in the Melbreak country) had chosen to lie-up for the day, wondering if he would ever see his game 'laal' terrier again.

He needn't have worried though, as Jack eventually found the fox and quickly bolted it, which must have delighted, if not surprised, those in attendance, making Jack a legend in his own lifetime, as any terrier successfully working foxes out of places like Broad How, would very quickly earn a reputation as a great worker and would be bred from on a large scale. Jack would greatly influence the future breeding of Lakeland stock and his line would undoubtedly have continued in the Ullswater bloodlines in particular, though no doubt other fellpacks of the time made use of the stud services of this game and reliable terrier. Incidentally, that fox then made for Tongue Earth at Troutbeck Park and was bolted again, before going to ground once more at Kentmere, where it was finally dug out and killed.

Another legendary terrier was Rock, which had carved out a reputation as a first class worker by the early 1860s. Exactly how Rock was bred is impossible to say, but he may well have been bred out of the old Melbreak bloodlines, which even so early on were producing quite typey terriers with good coat and colour. A red strain was being produced at the Melbreak in those days, which were excellent workers. Rock was owned by Mister Irving, who owned and hunted the Maryport Otterhounds, which pack hunted much the same country as the Melbreak Foxhounds.

Friday April 3rd 1863 witnessed the Maryport Otterhounds meeting at

Broughton Bridge near Cockermouth, with a start made at 7am. Hounds were drawing the River Derwent – a river beloved by William Wordsworth, the famous Lakeland poet, and after a long draw Careless, Swimmer and Stormer, three of his best hounds, finally roused an otter. After a long hunt Ruby and Stormer marked a holt by the riverside and Ruby managed to reach the otter and pulled it out, but it shook itself free and went further upstream, before going to ground once again. Sailor marked this time and so Irving, on arriving with the terriers, elected to give Randy a try, but he proved a little too big and couldn't quite get up to the otter. Thus Rock was given a go and he really got at his quarry, in spite of the fact that this was a very tight holt. Rock wouldn't give ground and stayed at the otter, having to be dug out some time later, when it was discovered that Rock was in a fearful state, having been mauled quite badly by the otter. Mister Irving asked one of the followers to carry Rock home for treatment, while the hunt continued, the otter being drawn by Stormer. Poor Rock sadly died of his injuries, but only after he had become a sort of canine celebrity in the Lake District, due to his incredible abilities at work. Before his demise, however, Rock stamped his type and abilities into several progeny and traces of his bloodlines undoubtedly still exist today.

Ullswater Pinch was another grand terrier which became a legend in the Lake District during the 1890s, when Joe Bowman was hunting hounds. He was around at the same time as another great worker, Ullswater Jack, which, as my research indicates, was a white terrier. This is most interesting, as it was previously thought that the first white terrier to work at the Ullswater was Lil, a bitch Jonathan Wilkinson, the father of Sid and Joe Wilkinson, bought in North Yorkshire in 1907 – possibly from the disbanded Wensleydale pack which hunted fox, as well as hare. Pinch, described as one of the best and gamest terriers ever to go to earth, like Rock of the Maryport Otterhounds, was destined to die whilst at work. This was at a bad place under Gowder Crag, in the Haweswater area, after a meet at Shap in 1900.

It seems that Pinch found and engaged the fox (which was quite a feat in this huge earth), but this rock earth being as vast as it was, two other terriers, Punch and the famous Jack, were also to ground. All three terriers got at the fox, but on digging down to the scene of the encounter and breaking through, it was discovered that Pinch had died while still hold of the fox. Exactly how is not known, but my guess is that Pinch suffocated in that crowded tight space. Jack and Punch were fine, having worried the fox below.

These are just a very few of the large number of game terriers which laid the foundation for our modern working strains, which have produced some incredibly efficient workers across the decades. In some countries working our terriers is rather restricted to say the least, but we must still aim to produce game workers which can live up to the reputations of their utterly superb ancestors.

35: MIDDLETON'S TEDDY – A LUNESDALE LEGEND:

One of the best working terriers to come from the early stock of a strain of Lakeland terrier emerging out of Gary Middleton's breeding programme was a dog named Teddy, which was owned by one of Middleton's digging friends. Gary described Teddy as probably the best finder he had ever seen at work and, though Gary bred him, Teddy was owned and mostly worked by Arthur Wells. Teddy was out of Gary's strong and utterly game bitch, Rags – a bitch with a magnificent head she inherited from Wilkinson's Rock – a terrier which, according to Gary, had a "'ead like a brick." The sire of Teddy was Rip, a gamekeeper's terrier used at fox on the wilds of Shap Fell, which Gary believed was bred out of Cyril Breay stock. My research confirms that most of the terriers serving with the gamekeepers of this and neighbouring districts in those days were bred from Cyril Breay's strain. In fact, Breay often accompanied such keepers on fox control hunts in this area, where they would often patiently track foxes in the snow, for miles and hours at a time, before following their prints to some lair, very often a rock earth or rockpile. Working silently, so as not to alert their fox as to their presence above ground, Breay would loose his terrier and wait patiently, alongside the keeper, for the fox to bolt. Breay, or the gamekeeper, would then shoot the fox as it fled from the earth, very often after a spectacular bolt – a very effective form of predator control and one still employed today.

 The gamekeepers of this area often went to Cyril Breay to obtain the very best workers and Rip was undoubtedly of this breeding and had proven most useful – useful enough for Gary Middleton to use Rip on his Wilkinson's Rock bred bitch, Rags, which had also proven very game at both fox and badger (badger digging was legal in those days). Rip was another grand worker, but Teddy was even better. Teddy, having already proven himself a very good worker by the beginning of the 1970s, was loaned to Barry Todhunter when he began whipping-in at the Lunesdale Foxhounds during the early 1970s, in 1971 to be exact. Barry hadn't seen Teddy at work before this time, but he was most impressed after Teddy went to earth on a fox that had been run into a bad shake-hole (pronounced 'shak-hole' in the fells) near Malham in the Yorkshire Dales. The terrier succeeded in bolting this fox from an earth which can easily and accurately be described as a death-trap. Some of the earths foxes inhabit in the Yorkshire Dales and the south-eastern fells of Cumbria can only be described as horrific places to put a terrier, as some lead to underground streams or brooks which can plunge for hundreds of feet into the darkest depths of the earth, or they link up with other water-moulded passages which can run through as many as three counties (Cumbria, North Yorkshire and North Lancashire). Terriers lost in such places have very little chance of ever emerging, let alone working foxes out of such nightmare earths in the first place. Teddy had done incredibly well to successfully bolt a fox from a rocky lair of this type, as the ground beneath Malhamdale is full of death-trap rock dens where foxes seek sanctuary when pressed by hounds.

Teddy's forte', however, was when he worked a fox out of a bad place in the shadow of Pen-y-gent near Horton in Ribblesdale in North Yorkshire. In fact, this earth was considered an 'impossible' place for terriers, as terriers had been lost here during previous hunts in the area, but Teddy slipped his collar after hounds ran a fox in and marked the earth eagerly. George Perfect, the gamekeeper of this district and a man who was a famous character in the north, warned Barry not to put his terrier to ground here, so his heart sank when Teddy got loose and ran to earth in pursuit of the hunted fox. Teddy then quickly disappeared into the rock earth and Barry feared the worst would happen, as, two hours later, nothing had happened nor was there any sound from the dark recesses of this vast and dangerous earth. However, hoping for the best, Barry carefully listened and at last faint barking could just about be heard, which grew louder and louder as time passed. The fox then bolted at great speed, with Teddy emerging right on its brush, with hounds quickly off in pursuit of their quarry. Barry remarked that the sight of that fox, hunting hounds and chasing terrier, running across the wilds of the Yorkshire fell country was spectacular to say the least, the continuing hunt made all the more sweeter by the knowledge that Teddy, after all, was safely out of that death-trap earth. George perfect, a man who had hunted with the best of them, including Cyril Breay, Frank Buck and Walter Parkin, was full of praise for Teddy, as the earth he had successfully worked a fox out of, was a noted stronghold and a known death-trap for terriers. In fact, George Perfect had been quite certain that they would never see Teddy again after he had slipped his collar and gone to ground.

Teddy was just one of many top class workers Gary Middleton bred out of his Lakeland strain, which was based on Sid Wilkinson's Rock and a Dent strain of fell terrier Gary inherited from his Great Uncle Dick who farmed at Dent and who kept terriers about the farm for keeping predators away from his livestock. Gary was certain this strain would have been a mixture of old Lunesdale Foxhounds bloodlines bred by such notables as Walter Parkin, Jossie Akerigg and Cyril Breay, which type he improved using Rock bred terriers whose bloodlines were saturated with working registered Lakeland terriers. Through this breeding, as well as Rip, the sire of Teddy and other Middleton bred terriers, Cyril Breay bloodlines also entered the famous strain which produced working terriers of the calibre of Teddy, a Lunesdale legend.

☀

36: HISTORIC HUNTING IN THE LUNE VALLEY:

Old newspaper accounts reveal that a number of packs have hunted the Lune Valley across the centuries and one of these was the Oxenholme Harriers. They enjoyed a mammoth hunt at the beginning of the spring of 1890, after a meet at Kirkby Lonsdale. A deer was roused at Tunstall in the beautiful Lune Valley and she was one that had been hunted by these harriers on numerous previous occasions. The members of the hunt had even named the deer and she was affectionately known as 'Mabel.' The deer was 'put off' from the banks of the river Lune and a fast hunt followed, taking hounds all around this district and crossing the river twice, before heading north-east to Leck Beck. Their pilot kept to the course of the beck and into Easegill (a place hunted often by Cyril Breay, Frank Buck and Roger Westmorland), following the gill onto the wilds of lofty Leck Fell which is rich in hunting history, though usually with footpacks. The Oxenholme Harriers were a mounted pack and they struggled to follow hounds across the peat bogs and rush-beds of Leck Fell, just about keeping the tail-hounds in sight.

Hounds hunted their quarry right out and over the high fell tops over two thousand feet in height and into the next dale, eventually taking hounds right through the charming village of Dent, with the villagers joining in the chase, which was proving to be a screaming hunt, the cry of the pack echoing amongst the rocky outcrops of the surrounding fells. Twenty minutes or so later the field came riding through Dent Village and it says something for their resilience that they were able to follow the course of this hunt, which covered some incredibly rough and bog-strewn country.

The deer finally took to a deep pool on the River Dee and here she was taken up unharmed and undoubtedly later released back into the wild. What was left of the field then made their way to Sedbergh where refreshments were enjoyed and then hounds and hunt staff arrived back at kennels near Kendal, well after dark. It had been a long hunt that had taken in some of the worst fell country to cover on foot, let alone mounted on horseback, which was remembered as a real red letter day for the Oxenholme Harriers.

The Lunesdale Foxhounds have hunted much of the Lune Valley for several decades now and they too have enjoyed some great days, such as the time that a fox was roused near Bolton Le Sands, which took hounds through glorious rolling hill country on the western side of the Lune Valley and all the way to Hutton Roof, where the fox was either lost, or it went to ground, the details of the conclusion being a little scanty. Another grand hunt around Lord's Lot concluded with the fox going to ground on the railway embankment, which was dug out by a local farmer who kept and worked the old working terrier bloodlines bred by Cyril Breay, who was a regular follower of this hunt for many years.

Mart hunting packs were once common throughout the British Isles and they hunted mostly polecat with considerable success, though stoats were also hunted, with pinemartens being hunted wherever they could be found, such as in the Lake District. Accounts show that a mart pack operated in the northern fringes of the Lune Valley and there have been some great hunts at polecat and stoats. A mart was roused by a small mart pack on the lower reaches of Casterton High Fell and hounds struck its line and flew with a lovely cry up along a drystone wall, heading straight up the fell. The mart went over the wall and hounds soon followed, hunting the hot line to a tumbled part of another stone wall, where they marked eagerly. A terrier joined in the fray and, pushing its snout in amongst the stonepiles, succeeded in bolting the mart, which was hunted right up the fell and to the corner of the wall, where it swung to the right, following yet another wall which was built right across the middle part of the fell, leading to Easegill. Hounds flew, putting themselves right after a bad check, and finally marking the mart to ground once again, at a rock hole above a beck that fed another ghyll, not far from Easegill. In spite of the attentions of a keen terrier, the mart could not be bolted, nor could it be dug out, so it was left for another day.

Polecats, pinemartens and stoats, the main quarry of mart hunting packs which were common during the 19th century and early part of the 20th century, often got in among rocks and I have read an account of a hunt in the South Pennines area that started in pastures close to a quarry and ended, after a grand hunt, with hounds marking to ground in among the rocks of the quarry, with a long and hard dig following, till at last the mart, a polecat in this instance, was dug out and accounted for, though more often than not a mart had to be left and given best.

The Vale of Lune Harriers now hunt the Lune Valley (within the law of course) and have done so for the past 150 years. They now lay a trail for hounds, which they hunt well and with a very good cry, though some days are set aside for hound exercise, especially if the weather is not too favourable. At one time this pack hunted both fox and hare and some great days have been enjoyed in this most beautiful part of the world, which lies in North Lancashire, Cumbria and North Yorkshire. Truly, some great hunting has been enjoyed with various packs in the Lune Valley and Cyril Breay's game terriers also saw much service in this area.

37: TERRIER RESCUE – WITH THE LATE GARY MIDDLETON:

The late Gary Middleton bred and worked terriers for well over half a century and, as one can imagine, he had a wealth of experience when it came to the working of large quarry, particularly foxes and badgers, for Gary lived through a time when badger digging was legal. Inevitably, as is the case for anyone who works terriers on a regular basis, there would be times when his terriers came unstuck and this chapter discusses a few of the dramatic rescues that involved Gary Middleton and his game Lakeland terriers – as famous for their working qualities as for their winning ways in the show ring.

One of the most dramatic rescues involved a bitch named Tiny, which was one of the early terriers in his strain – a bitch, in fact, which produced several puppies to Sid Wilkinson's extraordinarily good looking dog terrier, Rock. Tiny saw plenty of work to fox and badger in those days (1960s) and one day he took this bitch with him whilst tracking foxes after a fresh fall of snow in the South Lakeland area. The fox prints led Gary and his hunting companion all over the area, but eventually they led into a rock earth that is situated close to the Sun Inn at Crook – a tiny village between Kendal and Bowness where Gary and Ruth, his wife, first set up home after their wedding. There has long been a tradition of tracking foxes in the snow and Jossie Akerigg of Garsdale was renowned for his skill and high success rate, as were Frank Buck and Cyril Breay, who, throughout their long lives, tracked foxes in the snow and bolted them to guns using their game terriers, or dug those which remained below ground.

No prints exited this rock den and so Gary loosed Tiny from the couplings and she entered the earth eagerly, yet carefully, as this was a tricky spot. Gary worked this place on a number of occasions and he stated that the rock formed a natural chimney, which dropped into the bowels of the earth to an unknown depth. Tiny managed to climb down into the rock crevice and soon found two foxes sheltering inside, which quickly bolted and were shot by the waiting guns, being killed instantly (although I have mostly either dug foxes, or bolted them to waiting lurchers or hound crosses, I have also taken part in this form of fox control on a number of occasions and can recommend it as one that is very effective indeed, though these days one must be aware of the law and try to keep on the right side of it when it comes to working terriers).

Gary soon realised that Tiny was in trouble, being unable to climb out of that slippery den, which demonstrates just how agile foxes are. He did his utmost to cajole her out of there, but she simply could not get enough grip to pull herself out, so Gary was forced to ponder the matter, finally coming up with an idea a couple of days later. He cut a lengthy bough from a nearby yew tree and then dropped it down the naturally formed chimney, being careful not to crush his little bitch whilst doing so. Having done this, Tiny began making attempts to climb out and eventually made progress after digging her dew claws into the rough bark and pulling herself up. She finally made it out and Gary was relieved, as one can imagine. Had this attempt failed, then a long and gruelling dig would have been necessary, and even then the outcome would have been uncertain.

Another rescue involved a terrier named Rags, which was a bitch bred out of Tim, who was in turn sired by Sid Wilkinson's Rock. Rags had a massive head and she became a famous fox killing bitch during the earlier years of Gary's breeding programme, but on this occasion it looked as though Rags would be lost forever. Gary had taken part in a dig near Cockermouth and the earth proved to be enormous. The place was so deep, in fact, that Rags could not even be heard, despite obviously being at her fox. This was long before locators came on the scene and the digging was merely guided by educated guesswork. Over several days, much digging by hand ensued, but then a digger was called in, which moved tons of earth and rock, but without success. No trace of Rags could be found, no sound could be heard and Gary now feared the worst, preparing himself to call a halt to operations, which he now deemed futile. However, an old chap visited the site with his faithful Jack Russell by his side and enquired as to what was going on. He then took his terrier to the site and it dug into the wall of the dig. The old gent assured Gary that his terrier was on the right track, and so digging began once again.

After they had dug into the bank to a depth of six foot, they uncovered a dead half-eaten fox. And then Rags, as fat as a pig, walked out of the tunnel as though she had only just entered, the diggers breathing a large sigh of relief. She couldn't see properly for a day or two afterwards, but otherwise Rags was in fine fettle.

On another occasion Gary was hunting a valley near Preston when he put a son of Old Rex, also named Rex, to ground in an earth with sandy soil around the entrance, which slightly worried him. Rex found and engaged his fox, which wouldn't bolt, so Gary and his companion began digging, coming upon almost pure sand a few feet into the dig. Freddie Hoyle was inside the hole, digging on to Rex, when the top of the dig collapsed, but thankfully Gary managed to pull him free rather rapidly. They then carefully cleared a way to Rex and his fox, which, it was discovered, had also been buried by collapsing sand. However, they pulled dog and fox clear. Both had suffered, but were still alive. Rex normally killed his foxes quickly, just like his famous sire, but the lack of air hampered him greatly during that dig, which almost ended in tragedy. Just a few minutes longer and no doubt the outcome would have been very different.

These are just a few of the exciting digs and rescues which Gary Middleton took part in throughout his long and eventful life. He was a traditionalist who believed that foxes had to be controlled for the sake of farmers in particular, and so his terriers were often put into places which would terrify many terrier men. Mostly his terriers worked such places successfully, occasionally coming unstuck and getting trapped. He lost very few terriers, however, simply because Gary was very careful about where he put his dogs, as well as his determination to rescue them whenever they did become trapped to ground.

38: JACK RUSSELL TERRIERS AT WORK:

I have enjoyed some great hunting days with Jack Russell terriers and one of the hardest digs I ever took part in to a Jack Russell terrier was on a lowland farm where several chickens had been taken by foxes. Barry and I had a look around the farmland, which was quite a large area, but we eventually located an earth where the remains of a number of the missing chickens were found. This was well into May, during the early 1980s, at a time when I kept, worked and bred Jack Russell terriers, not for show, but entirely for work.

This was a weekday, so our other digging partner, Roy, was at work and could not attend, so his bitch Judy, a daughter of my own bitch, Pep, wasn't in attendance either. However, Pep was a game little worker to fox and I was confident that she would be more than capable of handling this situation, should the earth prove occupied. My lurcher marked alongside Pep and so we had a good look round and located an exit hole on the other side of what was a farm track leading between two fields, with ditches at either side for drainage of the surrounding pastures. This broad farm track had been left and reinforced when the drainage ditches were dug out several years earlier, so I wondered how on earth we were going to tackle this dig.

I didn't want to bolt any of the foxes out of this earth, as the ground was very difficult and my lurcher and greyhound would have had little chance of a successful catch, so I determined to dig this den from the outset and with this in mind entered Pep, who went to ground with her usual eagerness. It was obvious a litter of cubs was in this earth, but whether or not the vixen was with them was as yet unknown, though well grown May cubs are often left to it once the vixen has fed them, so I would not have been surprised if just the cubs were in residence.

Pep had a little difficulty getting on, so I dug a little out of the entrance area and uncovered the fat carcass of one of the chickens which had recently been running around the farmyard and providing fresh eggs. Typically, the head was gone, together with much of the breast meat. Feathers poured out of the earth, but at last Pep got on and very soon she began baying strongly. I do not wish to bore anyone with lengthy detail, suffice to say that the digging was incredibly difficult and we could only go so far, so as to avoid compromising the integrity of the farm track above. We dug into both sides and our efforts took hours of hard toil, till it was obvious we could not reach the litter. It seemed that Pep couldn't get right up to them either, so I decided to block in the litter and return with Roy and his little bitch, Judy, which could get into tight places much better than her dam, due to her smaller and more slender size. Pep wouldn't leave her quarry, so I was forced to block her in too. I used old bricks and stones dug out of the embankment and jammed them in tightly, while making certain air could still flow through the earth.

On returning with Roy Pilling and his terrier bitch, Judy, it was discovered that the vixen had not been to ground after all, as she had managed to dig a tight space around the bricks and stones, giving her cubs enough room to exit their den and escape. Pep was waiting behind the bricks and stones at the hole at the other side of the earth, as she was unable to get right through, and finally walked out into the fresh air after spending twelve hours to ground.

Another dig involving Pep was only a few fields away from this earth, which was more successful. The weather had turned bitterly cold and often foxes will seek sanctuary from the elements below ground, so that February morning Merle, my lurcher, and Pep marked the entrance to a stone drain in low lying land and in Pep went, quickly finding and pushing the fox along the drain towards a stop-end. There was only one way in and out of here, so Merle was kept near the entrance in case of a bolt, while I went off to locate Pep, whose steady bay could be heard close to a tree.

That fox was not for moving, so I began digging, removing squares of turf until I had enough exposed soil to make sure the dig was roomy enough, but it was far from easy going. The first few inches were frozen pretty solidly and one of our spades finally gave up and snapped in half. After much perseverance, however, we finally broke through about three or four feet down, right on top of the fox, but I couldn't get hold of it, so Merle was used to grab and draw what turned out to be a fine dog fox in superb winter condition. However, we were pleased to account for it, as livestock worrying had been a problem yet again in this area. I did have some good photographs of Pep and Merle with this fine dog fox, but they have been lost over the years, probably when I got married and moved out of the family home.

One hunt which convinced me I needed harder terriers was one day when we were up on the high moors of the West Pennines, with a fox to ground in a spot which led under a line of crags that had been blackened during the days of heavy industry, when hundreds of chimneys once endlessly belched out black, acrid smoke into the surrounding areas.

Pep and another Jack Russell named Penny, bayed steadily and tried to shift the fox, but it found a good strong vantage among the rocks and refused to budge even an inch. After a lengthy attempt to persuade that fox to bolt to the waiting running dogs, we were forced to give it best and leave it to ground unmolested. A harder terrier would have killed it inside the earth, which was important in this sheep rearing area, which was why I eventually abandoned Jack Russell terriers for fell, Lakeland and Patterdale terriers. Nevertheless, we still had some great days with Jack Russell terriers, many of which were very successful.

39: HISTORIC TERRIER WORK:
Wednesday June 26th 1895 saw the West Cumberland Otterhounds

enjoying a meet at Ouse Bridge, close to where Tapster, one of their best hounds, marked a weir. Twist and Metz where put in and they drew him, with a good hunt following up the river and to a deep pool below the railway bridge at Portinscale;` later to become the home village of Douglas Paisley and his working strain of Lakeland terrier, as well as Bob Gibbons, yet another important breeder of early Lakeland terriers. The otter got into the roots of a tree here and climbed to a dry holt above the water. One of the terriers quickly bolted the otter and a long two-hour hunt ensued before Tapster forced him to dive. However, Tapster managed to get hold of the otter by the neck and held it until the others came up, killing a 16 pounds dog otter. The West Cumberland Times reported the hunt the following Saturday.

An interesting report appeared in the West Cumberland Times in the September of 1887 when a drunken fellow was walking the streets of Maryport with his terrier, which in typical terrier fashion had a go at a large dog that was muzzled, barking and biting. The owner of the terrier kicked the big dog, so a doctor who had been watching the unfolding events from his window came outside and kicked the terrier. The owner of the terrier then struck the doctor and the doctor hit back. A proper fight broke out, but the doctor's wife managed to stop it. Just like a little belligerent terrier to start all of that trouble that made the local papers, though nobody ended up in court.

Another article of interest to terrier enthusiasts appeared in the same newspaper in the December of 1886, which gives us an insight into just how popular rabbit coursing competitions with terriers was in those days. The report informs us that a fox terrier named Timp was unbeatable at rabbit coursing. The terrier won all over England at competitions held under the strictest rules of the Liverpool Coursing Club and one disgruntled competitor tried to get the terrier banned after winning once again at Egremont, claiming that it wasn't pure-bred. His efforts failed, of course, and Timp's reputation continued to grow.

During the 1890s the West Cumberland Otterhounds drew the river Ehen from Sellafield to Egremont with not a trace of scent, but then hounds struck a drag and stuck to it, to a holt in among tree-roots where they marked-in. Terriers Grip and Twist were put in and they were hard at him for quite a lengthy time until, finding the terriers to be more than a handful, he decided to bolt. Hounds then had a terrific hunt of four hours and finally caught and killed him. Twist and Grip were both badly mauled during the encounter underground, having never flinched in a very difficult holt to work. The game pair of working terriers had to be carried home for treatment. The otter weighed 25 pounds. Present were Mr J. Longmire, J. Irwin, Mr Dixon and many followers from Egremont and Whitehaven.

I have also found an interesting article that appeared in the Aberdeen Evening Express on Wednesday December 7th 1887, regarding the son of that famous huntsman, John Peel. Much has been written about John Peel senior, but very little regarding his offspring. This son of the 'Auld' huntsman was named after his father and he also hunted all his life, mostly mounted, though he undoubtedly also followed the fell-packs on foot, hunting until he was 88 years of age, when he could no longer get on a horse. Young John Peel, as he was known, died just two years later at the age of 90, having been able to blow his father's hunting horn almost to his last breath.

Snooty was a working terrier belonging to J. Oakes of Swinscoe in Derbyshire and in 1956 the terrier was put in a small hole during a fox shoot. A fox quickly bolted and was shot, but only wounded, so it turned and went back in the same earth. Snooty bolted it once again and this time the fox was shot and killed, but the terrier failed to emerge. What followed was three days and nights of hard digging, an earth-mover being brought in, as the den proved to be very deep. The digger worked to a depth of twenty-foot and the terrier was eventually uncovered forty-foot from the entrance. Thankfully, Snooty was in good shape.

In Glamorgan a large stoat entered a woman's bedroom and the August 1921 newspaper dramatically reported that it went for her throat. She obviously cornered it and all members of the Marten family will attack if cornered. The stoat got in behind a chest and a local terrierman was sent for. His terrier quickly engaged the stoat and killed it after a bit of a fight. This was a wire-haired fox terrier and in those days many were still worked. I can remember Neil Wilson telling me about a fisherman on the Isle of Mull who had a mink on his boat. Like the woman just mentioned, he cornered the mink and it attacked him. The Marten family are certainly not short on guts and it takes a game terrier to tackle them.

40: WORKING TERRIERS & LIVESTOCK BREAKING:

Simply put, breaking working terriers, or any breed of working dog come to that, to livestock is an essential part of their training, which must not be neglected. I am not here speaking from some pedestal as though I know it all – not at all (I have kept working dogs now for well over forty years, yet

I am still learning all the time), but I am speaking from experience. My bitch Beck was such a meek and mild little terrier that, as she was maturing, I sort of neglected the breaking to livestock part of things simply because she seemed totally uninterested in chasing anything but legitimate quarry. Her brother Turk, on the other-hand, was very headstrong as a youngster and so I put hours of livestock breaking into his training programme, which paid off. The number of times he has flushed or bolted foxes and gone off hunting his quarry right through flocks of sheep are innumerable and even though he would often be well out of sight I could trust that he would not take to chasing sheep or any other livestock.

One day when out on the high moors and I was drawing large rush-beds for foxes with a pack of terriers, a sheep got up right in front of Beck and I was horrified to see her give chase. I put on the sternest voice possible and this proved to be enough to stop her after a few yards of weakness, but she should never have given chase in the first place. All the other terriers remained completely steady. It was then that I realised I had put most of the livestock training into Turk and had neglected to give proper attention to this aspect of training with regard to Beck. I quickly put that right and Beck was then given an intensive training session which worked. She never again even thought of chasing livestock, but turned away with a complete lack of interest, even if a sheep ran right in front of her.

Before livestock training can begin there is one element in the rearing of a puppy that will greatly assist the success of such training, and that is good early socialising. The more contact a puppy has with people, including children, and other dogs, the more biddable a working terrier will be. And this can be true of terriers reared in kennels too, which generally do not have as much contact with people as those which 'live in.' The biddable nature of terriers was brought home to me one day when I was out with the Blencathra Foxhounds which were hunting the Walla Crag area east of Derwentwater; a stone's-throw away from Keswick. Hounds soon roused a fox at this 'smittle' (Lakeland terminology for a place that often holds a fox) spot and were away from their huntsman, Barry Todhunter, very quickly, with the huntsman's terriers eagerly following. Barry simply shouted "terriers" in a stern voice and immediately stopped them in their tracks. They then turned-tail and returned to his side. That is great control of a notoriously strong-willed breed of dog and such control can only be accomplished through good early socialising.

Good basic training will help a growing puppy to learn to respond to its master's commands and by the time vaccinations are completed a puppy will usually be responding to such commands as 'sit' and 'lie-down,' perhaps even the 'stay' command. Once it is safe to walk your puppy after vaccinations are completed, livestock training can begin. One can do this from footpaths bordering farmland if the livestock is close enough, but it is always best to get into the fields and walk through livestock on a regular basis. This means getting permission from a farmer, though nowadays a lot of livestock is grazed on common land where open access is the norm'. Just a word of caution, however, never walk through cattle where there are also calves, as cows are very protective and can stampede when dogs are in the same field as their youngsters (if ever in a field where cattle do charge, let your dog loose, as the cows are only trying to see off the dog and will chase it. Dogs can easily get out of the way). Be wary of bulls too, as well as some horses, which can be very aggressive towards dogs. We will here concentrate on breaking to sheep, but the principles are the same for all livestock training.

More diligence is needed when it comes to sheep, as these are incredibly nervous creatures which almost invite dogs to chase them, due to the often hysterical way in which they behave. Walking through sheep with your terrier on a short lead is the best method, as then it is easy to jerk the dog back if it shows any inclination to give chase, or even shows a slight interest in the sheep. Your goal is to get your terrier to completely ignore sheep.

Sternly warn it to 'leave' whilst jerking back the lead and this should work with the meeker, milder sort. However, many terriers are incredibly headstrong and will put up for 'boss' on an all-too-frequent basis. You must be firm. To establish your role as pack leader, make certain that at home you are boss and do not allow your dog to ignore any command. Also, do not allow it to go through doors or gates ahead of you in anything other than a working setting. This helps establish the dog's place in your family arrangement, which should always be subservient to the human members (in a kind, but firm manner, not a bullying, domineering manner). This will then help a headstrong dog to still be biddable. Be regular at breaking to sheep, but keep the sessions short and always give praise when your terrier responds positively, even giving little treats such as milk drops if you prefer. By the time it is ready to begin work your terrier should ignore sheep and show no interest in them whatsoever. For the more headstrong, cracking a leather lead on the ground in front of your terrier if it shows any inclination to give chase will usually work. This distracts the thoughts of your terrier and helps it to change tack, so to speak.

I have enjoyed great success at livestock breaking, only having a couple of mishaps; the one mentioned and once when Rock weakened and snapped at ducks she was chasing rats through (though I suspect that was more from frustration because they were getting in her way!). Bracken, my working basset-hound cross has been the most difficult of my dogs to break to sheep, so when a youngster I coupled him to Turk and Beck so that he learnt from their solid example, which complimented his regular training sessions. Youngsters learn much from older, steadier working dogs.

Those of us who provide farmers with an effective and free form of pest control are doing a good job, there can be no doubt about that, but it is essential that we have well behaved and trustworthy working dogs. Diligence when it comes to breaking to livestock will bring such desired results.

41: THE JOHN COWEN STRAIN OF LAKELAND TERRIER:

The late John Cowen was one-time terrierman to the Melbreak Foxhounds and during those many years he bred some of the best working Lakeland terriers ever produced, both from a working and exhibiting point of view, as Cowen's stock won well all over the country and descendants of his strain still produce excellent working and showing stock today.

His foundation stock was a mix of Harry Hardisty strain fell terriers, bred partly out of Willie Irving stock, and Lakeland terriers bred by Arthur and Harry Irving which were originally bred out of Willie Irving strain Lakeland terriers. With such a mix as this, it is not surprising that John Cowen went on to breed some of the best working and looking Lakeland terriers ever. To illustrate just how useful such foundation stock was, we must take a trip back to the early days of Cowen's time acting as terrierman to the Melbreak Foxhounds and to a terrier Cowen obtained from Harry Irving during the 1950s. This terrier was Mac.

Mac was a good looking dog with a tight, harsh Lakeland terrier coat and one day a fox was run into a tight spot on Low Fell by the Melbreak Foxhounds. John was asked to try Mac as these Lakeland terriers descended from Irving stock were usually narrow in the chest and were thus able to negotiate tight places. The only trouble was, Mac had never been to a fox before and so Cowen was a little nervous about using him, lest he failed to enter on that occasion (some terriers, no matter how well bred they are, do not always go to the first fox they see). John loosed his young terrier and Mac entered the earth, pushing on through the tight places and getting right into the earth. There was a little bit of noise during Mac's stint to ground, a bit of a scuffle between terrier and fox being obvious, but a few minutes later Mac emerged without any sign of a bite, or even a slight scratch.

John was a little embarrassed when some in the crowd who were watching on began to ridicule his dog, writing it off as "useless," but Willie Irving, having recently retired as huntsman and knowing this strain of terrier inside-out, having bred this strain from about 1916 onward, stated that Mac had killed the fox below. No one believed Irving, not even Cowen himself, as there had been little noise when Mac was below ground and he had emerged very soon after going to ground unmarked. Irving was adamant that Mac had killed that fox, but even so an unbelieving Harry Hardisty asked that another terrier be tried and it went to ground and pulled out a stone-dead fox, which Mac had indeed finished. There was silence among the once-mocking crowd for several moments afterwards.

John brought on Mac and he served for a short while with the Blencathra Foxhounds on loan to Johnny Richardson, before being passed on to Tom Robinson who whipped-in at the Melbreak for a number of seasons. Tom used Mac on any lamb or poultry worrying foxes which were not required to be bolted. Mac finished his foxes incredibly quickly and avoided serious injury whilst doing so. This strain of terrier produced several terriers capable of such feats and that is why Willie Irving had been so confident that Mac had killed that first fox he entered to.

John bred several of his terriers out of Harry Hardisty's good looking dog, Turk, and one memorable hunt was yet again on Low Fell. Hounds marked an earth and Turk was entered, engaging his quarry, but it soon became obvious that it wasn't for bolting. Hardisty moved on to try for another, while John Cowen began digging. He eventually reached Turk, which had bottled-up four large badgers, which erupted from the tunnels after Cowen broke through, all four badgers milling around his feet. Incidentally, Turk was bred out of a granddaughter of Jim Fleming's Myrt. Myrt, in turn, was bred by Willie Irving out of his Melbreak Turk line. Cowen's strain was saturated with Turk's bloodlines and consistently produced excellent working stock.

One of Cowen's best dogs bred out of Turk was his famous Rock. The Melbreak Foxhounds and their huntsman Harry Hardisty were staying at John Cowen's farm at Embleton and that morning they were hunting the fells opposite the farm. One of the bitches, Welcome, began marking an earth on the fellside and Cowen put in his dog Rock. There was not a sound from this obviously deep lair and after several moments John decided to put in one of his bitches, as Rock may have been struggling to pin-down his quarry if the earth was huge. Two foxes bolted soon after and the pack split, hunting both. His bitch then settled on a third fox and Cowen dug to her. He then uncovered Rock, who was grimly hanging onto a fourth fox in spite of being in rather an awkward position. Rock was incredibly game and produced both excellent working and good looking stock.

To further illustrate the gameness of Cowen's terriers, we must go back to Mac. This terrier once took a severe mauling from a badger which was lurking inside a fox earth marked by hounds. A week or so later a fox was run to ground and several hunt terriers were tried, but it was in such an awkward spot that none could do a thing with it. Hardisty, knowing Mac's abilities, finally asked John to try him, but his wounds hadn't quite healed properly from his encounter with Brock a week before. However, Cowen was a traditionalist who knew hunting in the fells was about controlling foxes, not sport, so he agreed in the end and loosed his terrier. Mac must have been an exceptionally game dog, as only ten minutes after being loosed, he emerged from the earth and the fox was dead.

Another grand terrier was Rebel. John was out with the Blencathra Foxhounds when Bill Porter was whipper-in and a fox was run to earth on Binsey Fell, which featured in many of John Peel's hunts and a fell he named one of his ponies after. Bill Porter entered one of his rough-haired crossbred bitches. She later emerged, unable to shift the fox, so Cowen was asked to try Rebel. Rebel was keen to get and soon found and engaged his fox, persuading it to bolt soon after. Unfortunately, Rebel was lost to ground at Millson Moor after a fox was holed by hounds. The dig lasted for three days and a number of badgers were dug out during that time, but Rebel was never seen again. John surmised that his dog had attacked a badger as he would a fox and was killed in the scuffle.

John Cowen bred dozens, if not hundreds, of great working terriers which also showed themselves well across the several decades that he worked them. Many strains are descended from his stock and Colin Armstrong of West Cumbria continues to breed a relatively pure line which he has worked throughout the Lakes and the Borders of Scotland, where he carries out fox control for gamekeepers. John Cowen was yet another of the great Lakeland terriermen who have bred sound stock that produces our working terriers of today. In fact, there are few working terrier strains of today that are not at least in-part bred form the excellent terriers produced by John Cowen of Embleton.

42: HISTORIC HUNTING WITH HOUNDS & TERRIERS:
Peter Ormrod of Garstang in Lancashire had many terriers from the great Arthur Heinemann of Devon, who bred a very game and sensible strain of Jack Russell terrier reputedly descended from Parson John Russell's

terriers. Heinemann was a great advocate of well organised badger digs in which both the terriers and badgers came out of unharmed, for Heinemann rarely killed badgers unless the landowner specifically requested that he did, as badgers can and do kill livestock such as lambs and chickens, and his terriers were very sensible and were rarely bitten during encounters with Brock. Ormrod had hunted alongside Heinemann and his testimony is fascinating. Writing in 1908, he stated that Heinemann's terriers were able to keep up with hounds on the wild and wide open spaces of Exmoor, were able to throw their tongues and push foxes out of the densest, deepest coverts, while also being able to get to ground, very often before hounds had reached the earth. He testified from experience that Heinemann not only looked after and treated his working terriers very well, but also that he treated his quarry with respect, dealing humanely with fox or badger. Surely modern working terrier enthusiasts can learn a valuable lesson from such excellent examples.

In the month of February, 1910, the Melbreak Foxhounds, still under the Mastership of Squire John Benson, who held this post for 51 years and who remembered hunting with the legendary John Peel, having vivid memories of seeing Peel in his 'Hodden' grey coat mounted on his best hunter, Dunny, enjoyed a good hunt around the picturesque Loweswater Fells and after hounds began pressing their fox hard, Jacky set his mask for the low country and sought sanctuary in the wash-house boiler at Mister Burnyeat's farm, Latterhead, the farmer closing the boiler door so that the fox could not escape. However, when one of the maid servants heard hounds approaching, she was heard to say "poor laal thing" and she then opened the boiler door, letting Jacky loose once more. The fox then swam the river Cocker, but was caught by hounds on the opposite bank after what had been a long and exciting hunt.

During the spring of 1908 a fox got in among turkeys, killing several in typical fox-fashion, and the Melbreak Foxhounds, hunted at that time by Jonathan Banks, a farmer whose farmstead was at the foot of Melbreak Fell, where hounds were also kennelled, were called in. Banks only had six hounds still in kennel, the rest having returned to their summer walks (a system still used by the fell-packs), so he turned out early morning with his reduced pack and they roused their livestock killing fox a few minutes after 7am. What followed demonstrates just how good Fell Foxhounds were when it came to hunting livestock-killing foxes, even with just a few hounds available, as a long and hard hunt began that saw hounds running over several fells and dropping down into the low country several times until, at last, the six hounds pulled their fox down in a farmyard at

Watergate at 7pm, just a few minutes short of twelve hours duration: an incredible achievement for just six hounds. A successful outcome was vital if the livestock worrying was to be put to an end.

Having mentioned Squire John Benson, it seems fitting to divulge a little more information regarding this sporting gentleman, who was extremely keen on fox and otter hunting, earning his living as a Cockermouth-based Lawyer. Not only did he take on the Mastership of the Melbreak Foxhounds for 51 years, but he also formed the West Cumberland Otterhounds and used Fell-Foxhounds in this capacity too, as he believed they were better at marking and quicker at hunting than otterhounds proper. His best hunt with this renowned pack was in the Coniston area when hounds hunted an otter for eight hours in total, hounds eventually catching a 25pound otter in Coniston Water. Squire Benson was from a sporting family, as his grandfather was once Master of the Cockermouth Harriers. When Squire Benson retired in 1917 he was interviewed by local newspaper reporters and it was discovered that he was the only person still living who had hunted with John Peel.

Some days with Fell-Foxhounds could be a very busy time for terriers. One such day was in February 1954. A fox was found and run to ground at Armaside Fell. Harry Hardisty was huntsman of the Melbreak Foxhounds at the time, having taken over from Willie Irving in 1951, and Harry had some excellent terriers, as did Cyril Tyson and John Cowen, who were doing much of the terrier-work for Hardisty in those days. A game terrier was put in and it killed the fox, so hounds were moved on. They marked an earth at Low Fell and the fox was bolted. A third fox was run into a badger sett at Waterloo and this too, bolted. And then fox number four was hunted and run into yet another badger sett, but it couldn't be bolted. The report didn't state the outcome, but I suspect terriers either killed the fox underground, or Jacky got in behind a badger and wouldn't bolt. A busy day for terriers indeed!

During January 1954 the Blencathra Foxhounds were staying at the farm of Mr & Mrs Tyson at Watendlath, when Johnny Richardson was in his early years as huntsman, for a week of hunting. They had a blank day on the Tuesday, as the weather was terrible, but the Thursday meet proved to be memorable indeed. Hounds roused a fox at Great End, which then took them down to the famous Bowderstone, then back up the fell and around Great End Crag, going to ground in a borran by the crag. Jacky was bolted and took hounds round Great End Crag again, then away for Blea Chag and to Comb Breast. The fox then made for Moss Mine and went to ground again. Terriers were entered and engaged their fox, but it wouldn't bolt and was worried-in, making this the sixty-first fox of the 1953/54 season.

That Walter Parkin was a much-respected huntsman of the Lunesdale Foxhounds is evidenced in the way people who remember him still talk about him, as well as the fact that local reporters also regarded him highly when writing about his many escapades with hounds and terriers. He was so highly respected, in fact, that Joe Bell of Orton named one of his terriers after him. 'Walter' was a very game fell terrier and when he was three years of age he was put into an earth at Asby Ghyll near Orton after a fox had been run-in by the Lunesdale hounds, during their last meet of the season, held on Easter Saturday in the April of 1960. Jewel was also put in and it soon became obvious that the fox wasn't going to bolt. Neither did the terriers emerge after a wait of some time, so digging commenced and Jewel was reached and rescued on the Sunday, but there was no sign or sound of Walter. Crowbars, sledgehammers, pick and shovel were used by Walter Parkin and a number of hunt followers, but progress was hard and very slow once hard rock was encountered. On the Tuesday Bill Greenhow, a Shap quarryman, was called in and he used gelignite to blast the hard rock, but even with such an extreme tool at their disposal, progress was still slow. During the following Saturday they finally broke through and Walter was found dead, alongside a dead fox, under a slab of solid rock at a depth of eight foot, twenty yards from where he had entered the earth. It seems that the terriers killed the fox and Jewel was on her way out when they reached her, while Walter became trapped on the other side of the fox and probably suffocated, as no serious injuries could be found. It is interesting to note that Ted Rigg, a long-time and well-respected breeder of pedigree Lakeland terriers, was whipping-in at the Lunesdale Foxhounds at this time, and did so for many years, though it seems on an amateur basis. Once their show careers were over, Ted Rigg liked to enter his charges to fox before breeding from them. Gary Middleton entered one of his champion dog terriers before putting him at stud and Gary found this Lakeland terrier to be very game, but not as sensible at work as his own unregistered Lakelands. It is not unreasonable to conclude that Rigg also used his Lakeland terriers at times with the Lunesdale Foxhounds and possibly with the North Lonsdale Foxhounds too, as he also followed this hunt.

During the spring of 1927, towards the close of Willie Irving's first season as huntsman of the Melbreak Foxhounds, a lamb killing fox was hunted and its cubs found, with just one being rescued from the attentions of the terrier. A cat belonging to Mister Swinburne of High Nook Farm near Loweswater had just lost its litter of kittens and so the cub was taken to the farm and put in with the cat, which adopted and raised it successfully.

Another hunt with this pack occurred in February 1909 after hounds had been unable to get onto the fells due to a week of hard frost, the pack being called out after several hens were killed by a fox at farms in the Loweswater area. The fox was found and hunted away from Low Fell, from Mister Swinburne's allotment to be precise, with Jacky taking them down by Oak Bank Farm, to Godferhead and onto Melbreak Fell. They then hunted to Mossdale Bottom, through Black Crag and to Carling Knott, where a second fox was roused, dividing the pack. The first fox took them down to Loweswater, past Mister Swinburne's High Nook Farm and to the shores of Loweswater where hounds pulled down a fine dog fox, swiftly ending the livestock losses in that area. The report didn't state what happened to the second fox.

That Fell-Foxhounds are incredibly tough animals can be illustrated many times over and in 1959 Tulip and Streamer were stuck for 27 hours on a ledge near the summit of rugged Honister Crag. These hounds were eventually rescued by Harold Tyson, Secretary of Cockermouth Mountain Rescue, and his colleague, Edward Ratcliffe.

43: HOBCARTON WHISK:

Whisk was born on January 2nd 1932 and he was registered as a pedigree Lakeland terrier under the name of Hobcarton Whisk by his owner, Willie Irving, on July 5th of that same year. Whisk was sired by Turk of Melbreak who was described by George Henry Long of Egremont as one of the hardest and gamest terriers ever to have worked with a fell pack. Peggy of Melbreak, bred by Jack Pepper of the Bowderstone kennels situated in the heart of the Borrowdale Valley, was the dam of Whisk and she was a sensible terrier which could both find a fox and finish it if need be. Willie also dug badger using this bitch, as she had sense enough to avoid severe maulings when at such testing quarry.

As far as records show, Hobcarton Whisk was entered to his first fox during a hunt with the Melbreak Foxhounds, the pack for which Willie Irving was huntsman, on February 7th 1933. The meet had been at Mockerkin Village and soon after being "lowsed" hounds struck a cold drag, which took them a fair distance all the way to Carling Knott, where two foxes were quickly afoot. The pack split and one lot had a good hunt over Hen Combe, Gale Fell, by Dodd, back by Tarn Crags and onto Gale Fell again where 'Jacky' went to ground. Reynard bolted very quickly after a terrier had been put in, but Willie watched as it dropped into another earth not too far distant.

He was soon with his hounds, which were now marking the earth eagerly, and he put in two of his terriers, one named Boss, which had some experience by this time, and Whisk, who was just over a year old. As far as I can tell, this was the first fox Whisk saw and he and Boss quickly found and worried the fox below ground, which was dug out by the followers. Irving went away after nine other hounds which hunted the other fox over into Ennerdale and killed at Mireside Garden. Boss had learnt his trade alongside Turk of Melbreak and Whisk began his career with Boss. It had been a good start for this game terrier and he then went on to become one of the gamest and most useful terriers of the 1930s – a terrier that could find in the deepest of earths and finish a fox single-handed.

Irving quickly began to rely on this terrier more and more and his next stint to ground of note was on March 27th 1933. Hounds had a fast hunt despite the dry and unusually warm conditions, with the fox going to earth at Wythop Hall Fell near Bassenthwaite Lake. Whisk was tried and he soon located his quarry, which wouldn't bolt. Willie dug out his terrier and Whisk had finished the fox by the time he was reached – no mean feat for a terrier that was barely over a year old and still inexperienced.

October 31st 1933 saw Whisk in action again, after hounds had been hunting foxes around woodlands situated close to the town of Cockermouth, from where Fletcher Christian of Mutiny on the Bounty fame hailed. The Melbreak had been in the Cockermouth area all week and their glorious music echoing about the woodlands had delighted locals and visitors alike. Hounds hunted one fox to Higham and on to Lowfield, where 'Jacky' holed inside a drain. Many of these Lakeland drains are quite vast in area and foxes can take some finding. Whisk was put to ground and after scrambling up the drain he found his fox and engaged it, but it wouldn't bolt because of being hard-pressed by hounds. Whisk and his quarry had quite a tussle in the darkness below, but the valiant terrier finished his fox and Willie dug them both out.

Willie Irving bred some incredibly good workers during his half-a-century or so of terrier breeding and during the 1930s he had several first-class working Lakelands on hand, whenever a fox went to ground. Roamer and Jewel were just two of these and they were bred exactly the same way as was Whisk, but from a later litter. Roamer went on to win several shows, but, like his sire, Turk, he became more of a legend for his working prowess. Like Whisk and Turk before him, Roamer could find and finish foxes single-handed and he did much work with the Melbreak pack. Whisk had the distinction of catching a fox above ground during a long hunt with the Melbreak.

The date was January 13th 1936 and by now Whisk was a seasoned worker. Hounds met at Lanthwaite Green and a fox was found at Rannerdale Knott, Buttermere. 'Jacky' led hounds on a long run over Whiteless, Grasmoor and Lad Hows, with their quarry then making for Coledale and over to Little Braithwaite, where Albert Thomas, the Whipper-in, viewed a weary fox. Albert unleashed Whisk and he quickly caught the fox, just before hounds at last arrived and accounted for their foe. Whisk was again to ground on February 3rd 1936 after a fox had been hunted from Dodd Fell to Brandlingill where it holed in a drain. Whisk quickly worried his fox before being dug out.

Irving didn't just breed game workers, but sensible ones too, as hunts with Whisk clearly demonstrate. After worrying that fox on February 3rd, Whisk was again put to ground on February 10th, just a week after killing a fox. Surely this is testimony enough that many of these early Lakeland terriers were not only great finders and game, but that they could handle their quarry with sense enough to avoid serious injury. That day hounds hunted all round woodland at Gilgarron, Jackie Planting and Winscales, where their fox ran in. Whisk was put in and he quickly worried a fox that wouldn't face hounds in the open again. Hobcarton Whisk was just one of many game terriers to have served with the fell packs of the Lake District and it is thanks to such great early breeding that we can produce equally good terriers today, though I would confidently state that terriers of such quality are much harder to come across these days than they were during the golden era of Lakeland and fell terrier breeding. The 1930s was a particularly prolific decade for producing excellent terrier stock and Hobcarton Whisk was just one of the incredibly useful terriers of that era. Whisk was used to ground many times and he worried more foxes than he bolted.

44: TERRIER RESCUE IN IRELAND:

Forty people were gathered on the hill in readiness of witnessing the final outcome of a terrier rescue that had begun five days previously, after Rusty had chased a fox into a pothole on Cregagh Mountain, two miles from Cushended in County Antrim, which is an area littered with such deadly places for working terriers. Frank Healy was a government fox hunter and he owned Rusty, though it was his son who was out hunting with the terrier at the time. A dozen diggers worked relentlessly from dawn till dusk each day and during operations they felled two trees, shifted a massive 300 tons of rock and dug a huge crater 30ft into the hillside, which was rather an inclement location at that time of year, December 1968. On the fifth day a massive seven ton boulder was shifted using block and tackle after a faint whimper had been heard and then one of the diggers, Robert McCallum, was lowered into the hole and he could see Rusty's nose at a very small hole, which he worked hard to enlarge until Rusty could get out. The large crowd, and especially the diggers, gave out a loud cheer as McCallum was lifted out with Rusty tucked under his harm, weak and a bit thinner, but nevertheless in reasonably good shape after being trapped for such a long time. Rusty was rescued 30 yards from the entrance and at a great depth. One can imagine the celebrations that took place that night!

Please note that the photos marked WTH are included courtesy of Working Terrier History Page admin. Many thanks for allowing me to use these photos.

Frisky being rescued in Staffordshire.

To ground with the Blencathra – 1950s, Johnny Richardson huntsman.

Harry Hardisty at the Melbreak kennels, WTH.

Blackstone Rock & Bella; part of the Blackstone District Ratchers Pack. Rock was trapped for 26hours after killing a fox and Bella located the earth. Myself and my brother dug her out.

George Chapman with Coniston Foxhounds and terrier, 1920s.

Johnny Richardson at the Blencathra.

Ullswater Foxhounds, George Salkeld, huntsman,
Braithwaite Wilson, whipper-in.

Carlisle Otterhounds & terriers, WTH.

George Chapman lifting the fox after being dug out of a borran, early 1920s, WTH.

Laal Tommy Dobson with two of his favourite Eskdale & Ennerdale hounds, WTH.

John Nicholson of the Lunesdale Foxhounds with Rusty, after a hard five-day rescue, 1950s.

To ground after a long hunt with the Coniston Foxhounds, 1921, WTH.

Tommy Dobson with his game terriers on the fells, WTH.

A Patterdale meet with the Ullswater Foxhounds, Auld Anthony Chapman 2nd from right, next to

huntsman Joe Bowman. Note the leggy terriers showing obvious Bedlington influence, WTH.

Auld Anthony Chapman with the Windermere Harriers. He was close friends with Tommy Dobson and, like Dobson, bred some very game terriers.

Otterhounds & terriers, WTH.

Harry Hardisty heading for the first draw after a meet at what looks like the Kirkstile Inn. Note the two terriers next to Hardisty. The one on the right is probably Turk, his most famous terrier, WTH.

Quality working terriers with the hunt

terrierman, WTH.

Frank Buck with Tex on his knee. Tex was an incredible working terrier with which Frank took hundreds of foxes, 1950s, WTH.

A kill with the Blencathra Foxhounds, 1930s, George Bell, huntsman, Albert Benson, whip. Benson's Red Ike was working with the pack at this time and ran loose with hounds. Walter Parkin based his terrier strain on Red Ike, the Ullswater strain and the terriers of Cyril Breay and Frank Buck, WTH.

Harry Hardisty with the Melbreak Foxhounds, 1950s. Tom Robinson was the whip, behind on right. I think the chap next to Robinson is a young John Cowen.

Anthony Chapman with Coniston Foxhounds & terriers.

*Ernie Parker with Coniston Foxhounds &
terriers. Parker whipped-in to Jim Dalton at
the 'Cathra before becoming huntsman at the
Coniston. He also worked as a shepherd for
Mrs Heelis (Beatrix Potter) at her Troutbeck
farm, WTH.*

*Willie Irving with Melbreak Foxhounds & terriers, very
likely late 20s or early 30s, Cockermouth, WTH.*

Walter Parkin with Lunesdale Foxhounds during their annual visit to Wensleydale & Bishopdale.

Keen badger digger of around 1900, WTH.

To ground with the Coniston Foxhounds, WTH.

My wife with Turk, Bracken & Beck in the
Borrowdale Valley, looking towards Skiddaw.

Badgers tailed at the end of the dig, WTH.

A badger dig, WTH.

Wastwater Taffy, 1930s, owned by J.J. Crellin, WTH.

Loweswater Show, 1930s, L-R Mrs Douglas Paisley, Kitty Farrer, Willie Irving & Alf Johnston of Oregill fame, WTH.

To ground in Wales, WTH.

Spider being handed over by Brait Black after she was rescued from a forty-foot crevasse on Pavey Ark, Langdales, in January 1934. Spider was freed on the 9th day. Two other terriers put in after a fox run to ground by the Coniston Foxhounds could not be rescued. The event made all the national papers and tourists flocked to the site to watch the rescue, with Brait Black leading proceedings, as he did on many, many terrier rescues in the Lakes.

Mrs Douglas Paisley with some of her husbands Registered Lakeland terriers, all of which served with the Blencathra Foxhounds for decades. They also worked otter and badger. This was taken in 1931. I think the terrier on the end, left, is Tinker, an incredible worker that served many bitches, WTH.

Willie Irving with the Melbreak hounds & terriers, Albert Thomas, whipper-in, 1930s. Whisk, Jewel & Roamer are very likely in the photograph.

Sir Jocelyn Lucas with his pack of Sealyham terriers, WTH.

George Bell & the Blencathra hounds & terriers at the Walla Crag meet, 1931, WTH.

To ground at Falcon Crag, near Walla Crag, in 1931, Blencathra Foxhounds, WTH.

To ground with the Ullswater Foxhounds. Anthony Barker is top left, WTH.

Hounds & terriers, WTH.

Printed in Great Britain
by Amazon